Biblical Proclamation for Africa Today

John Wesley Zwomunondiita Kurewa

Abingdon Press
Nashville

BIBLICAL PROCLAMATION FOR AFRICA TODAY

Library of Congress Cataloging-in-Publication Data

Kurewa, John Wesley Zwomunondiita.
  Biblical proclamation for Africa today / John Wesley Zwomunondiita Kurewa.
    p. cm.
  Includes bibliographical references and index.
  ISBN 0-687-01444-1
  1. Christianity—Africa, Sub-Saharan.   2. Bible—Evidences, authority, etc.
3. Bible—Homiletical use.   4. Preaching—Africa, Sub-Saharan.   5. Christianity
and culture.   6. Africa, Sub-Saharan-Religion—20th century.   I. Title.
BR1430.K87 1995
276.7'0825—dc20   95-21043
                                                                                      CIP

95 96 97 98 99 00 01 02 03 04—10 9 8 7 6 5 4 3 2 1
MANUFACTURED IN THE UNITED STATES OF AMERICA

Contents

Foreword

In sub-Saharan Africa, the second half of the twentieth century has been characterized by the expansion of missionary movements of the nineteenth century, struggle for political independence from colonial powers, and mobilization of efforts to build new, democratic African nations. John Wesley Zwomunondiita Kurewa is one of the witnesses of these events. He is not only an eyewitness of what happened or what is going on, but, like people of his generation, he also participated actively, from an African perspective, in evangelistic endeavors, political struggles for liberation, and the reconstruction of his nation. Dr. Kurewa assumed high responsibilities in his home church and in the department of evangelism in the World Council of Churches, where he became actively aware of the issues concerning evangelism, not only on the African continent, but also at the world level. He served as Secretary to the Parliament of Zimbabwe in the newly established nation of Zimbabwe before he assumed the responsibility of pioneering the office of Vice-Chancellor of a newly established United Methodist Church–related university in Africa.

Dr. Kurewa belongs to a generation of African intellectuals; or to be more specific, a generation of African theologians who live in a period of African history that can be qualified as one of transition. The wind of change, which brought and continues to bring transitions and mutations, started in the fifties at the height of African political consciousness, when only two countries on the whole continent, Liberia and Ethiopia, were independent. These intellectuals, in whatever country they live or work, are all convinced of their mission, which consists of examining, evaluating and even questioning every aspect of African colonial heritage including religion, culture, politics, and economy. In other words, this generation perceives its mission mainly as one of assisting the peoples of Africa to rediscover their soul in order to preserve their cultural identity in the modern world.

Anybody who has heard Dr. John Wesley Zwomunondiita Kurewa preaching, counseling, and teaching theology will recognize in the pages of this book the thread of his profound thought. In the flow of contemporary theological themes which are being discussed on the continent today such as Traditional Theology, Indigenized Theology, Black Theology, African Theology, Contextual Theology, Church and States issues, Authority and Power in Africa, the Gospel and Human Rights, the Family, and so forth, the thought expressed in this book stands between behavioral sciences and dogmatic theology. The contents of the book single out the uniqueness of the Bible in its composition, authority, transforming message, and unprecedented reputation. With the same intensity, the book underlines the necessity of bringing to the surface the values of African traditions and cultures that were submerged during the colonial period. The biblical proclamation, or what the New Testament varied writings call *kerygma,* includes both preaching and homiletics. If the first constitutes the task of delivering God's saving Word as revealed to the world through a preacher or messenger, the latter, however, provides rhetorical skills intended to make the biblical message communicable and audible in a given language. Authentic communication of the Word of God de-

pends, therefore, on the balance one makes between faithfulness to the Bible and deep understanding of an African
culture.

In looking at the title of this book an impatient reader may
ask to whom is this book primarily targeted? Well, the author
has called the addressee by his or her function, "the preacher
of the gospel." I would say that in addition to the preacher
(who may be understood here only as evangelist), any person
involved directly in pastoral ministry, especially in a congregation, will benefit much from the amount of information that
is given about the Bible and various methods of biblical
preaching in African situations. In this context the book is
recommended to church leaders, seminary lecturers, and
students alike.

Let me end this foreword by a short statement on what I
consider to be the main challenge posed by this book. Dr.
Kurewa has introduced to the preacher of the gospel the
importance of the Bible and the biblical proclamation for
today's Africa not only in theory, but also from his rich
experience in Christian ministry. The Bible, by its composition and contents, is a library in itself in many African families, especially in rural areas. It is my hope that the
encouragement which is given here to the preacher to maintain both the study of the Bible and African culture will open
to the reader a complex study of relationship between the
gospel itself and African cultural realities.

What this means, as the author has already indicated, is that
biblical preaching in Africa must strive toward understanding
the African cultural realities in order to communicate the
gospel effectively in the African situation.

D. K. Yemba
Dean, Faculty of Theology
Africa University
Mutare
November 1994

Preface

A t this time, when there are calls for the rewriting of the Bible, it is essential for preachers of the gospel to come to an understanding of the Bible's history, authority, and significance as the Word of God. Equally important is an appreciation of the role of culture in communication.

Some of our African cultural concepts could illuminate and enrich our understanding of the Christian faith, and the church in Africa today has a responsibility to study African culture in order to communicate the gospel effectively. To continue rejecting our culture in worship and theology will achieve nothing but the mutual alienation of our church and people. The gospel needs our culture for effective communication.

It is my hope that this book will enable preachers of the gospel to become diligent students of both the Bible and our African culture in order to become faithful proclaimers of Jesus Christ in Africa.

I am grateful to Professor Hoyini Bhila, Dr. Tara Elyssa, and Dr. Stephen Reed (both senior lecturers at Africa University) for reading the manuscript; to my secretary, Nyaradzo Madzongwe, for typing the final manuscript; and to my wife, Gertrude, for her encouragement as I worked on this book.

Chapter 1

African Experience
of the Bible

The Bible has exercised immense influence upon the life of the African people. The Bible has been translated into hundreds of African languages and dialects; and it may well be that it is the only book that many African Christian families possess. Indeed, the Bible stands as a powerful instrument of the Christian faith for the salvation of the African people from all sorts of diabolic powers.

From my years as a young rural pastor, I still recall how eager some older adult members of my circuit were to attend the literacy classes which were conducted in the church building. Their main reason for attending those literacy classes was to learn to read the Bible for themselves. The Bible has not only created a hunger of the spirit of people; it has also enabled the opening of eyes that were closed and blind for years, like Bartimaeus of Jericho in Jesus' time (Mark 10:46-52).

I also recall watching my late father—who had only three years of formal education, yet was a Methodist local preacher—reading his Bible at home. As his eyes began to fail him, he would ask one of the children to read some passages for him. If the reader stumbled on some word or phrase, my father was often able to name the word or correct the reader from memory. My father was a one-book man, and I never saw him read any book other than the Bible. He represents the many humble yet faithful Christians whose lives have been transformed by their faith in Jesus Christ. Reading the Bible daily, they live on his word.

Not long ago, I visited an older woman at her son's home on the outskirts of the city of Mutare. I had known the woman for many years since I grew up in the village where she lived, and she was a close friend of my parents. I remember many occasions when she came and prayed with my parents in our home. When I arrived at her son's place, I found her sitting outside in the shade of a tree, reading her Bible. During the conversation that ensued, she said that because she was no longer able to do any work in the fields or around the house, her main task, therefore, was eating and reading the Bible day and night. The nights were too long for her, so she shortened them by continuing her Bible reading. I consoled her by mentioning that my mother, who was about her age (95), was also engaged in the same business of eating, reading the Bible, and praying, even at midnight.

The same would be true of many older Christians in Africa today. Sons and daughters buy two or three Bibles for these older parents in a year. Some of these Bibles are actually worn out from daily use; others are simply misplaced, never to be found again.

On another day, I was traveling by bus from the Beit-bridge, a town on the Zimbabwean–South African border. A Bible salesman got on the bus with quite a few copies, and I bought two from him. An older woman who sat in a seat behind me started a conversation. She wanted to know what I was going to do with the two Bibles. When I told her that one was for myself and the other one for my mother, she was so grateful that I had been thoughtful enough to buy a Bible for my mother. She thought older people find more meaning in life by reading the Bible at a time when they seem to have nothing else to do. Clearly, Bible reading is regarded as the only satisfactory and meaningful activity by many older Africans.

However, the good book is not only for older people. I have seen many younger couples on their way to church, class meetings, or prayer meetings—carrying their hymnals and Bibles. This has been the case with the youth as well, as they go from one church to another for revival meetings and other events. They often have their Bibles with them; some read the Bible, while others simply carry it, but they all know that the Bible is an important book in a believer's life—the rule of faith and life.

I have been impressed by the fact that many members of the emerging, affluent, and literate generation of Christians in our African cities have an interest in the Bible. One might have suspected that they would be ashamed to be seen publicly carrying Bibles as they go to worship on a Sunday morning. No; they carry them, because they know the Bible is a good book. Among these young couples are business executives, medical doctors, architects, engineers, and other educated professionals. They carry their Bibles, and they read them, too. One cannot help thinking that all these different groups of people testify with the psalmist who said, "Your word is a lamp to my feet and a light for my path" (Ps. 119:105).

When we turn to the training program of the early African evangelists, or pastor-teachers as they were called in some churches, we find that their training from the outset had a special emphasis on the Bible. For example, in the Methodist Episcopal Church in Zimbabwe, now known as the United Methodist Church, by 1919 the emphasis in the training of pastor-teachers was on Bible study, memorizing scripture, and hymn-singing. The goal was to provide the pastor-teacher with biblical knowledge as a means of communion with God and, to some extent, to enable the preacher to learn how to "rightly [handle] the word of truth."

In the late 1950s, a missionary and teacher at Hartzell Theological Seminary told his class that systematic theology as a formal discipline had not been taught or taken seriously at that seminary until 1948, because the Methodist missionaries were not sure that Africans would grasp theological concepts. Hence the emphasis on biblical studies. Therefore, for good reasons or not, the Bible has had quite a long history at the center of the life of the African Christian. No wonder African preaching is often so biblically oriented.

The Reverend Bengt Sundkler, bishop in Bukoba, Tanzania, during the 1950s and 1960s, has shared his impressions of the African preaching tradition, which is deeply rooted in the Old Testament scriptures. He cites a typical incident in which a congregation of about five hundred, walking in a long procession, met at a cemetery in Natal on Easter morning. The preacher that morning, the Reverend Michael Mzobe, started his sermon with God's creation of heaven and earth. He proceeded to the creation of Adam and Eve, their fall, and the disaster of sin and death which came to the world as a result. In spite of the fall, Adam, after his death, was brought to Paradise where he was given a place of honor, seated alone on a balcony. From there, Adam witnessed human history. He watched his eldest son, Cain, murder his younger brother, Abel, in cold blood. Realizing that sin and death, which had come through him, had visited his descendants as well, all Adam could do was to cry, "My guilt, my great guilt!" He continued crying, asking God to help him overcome his sorrow.

The turning point of the sermon was the joy that came to the congregation as the Reverend Michael Mzobe described the joy that Adam must have finally experienced:

> Consider the incredible joy, that indescribable jubilation which filled Adam's heart on the First Easter morning, as the Hero of Heaven . . . came in through the Gate of Heaven, with His Crown of Thorns, now a brilliant Crown of Victory, walking the central aisle in the heavenly Temple, straight up to the Throne of the Almighty . There he gave his report that from this day Satan and Sin and Death had been overcome. For now

He, the Second Adam, had won the victory.
"And the First Adam had peace."[1]

African preachers have long been able to move and inspire
their congregations through the use of the Bible in their
sermons. Therefore, biblical proclamation is not a new thing
in the life of the African Church. Rather, it is the only way of
preaching that we know; and it is the only way of preaching
that was ever effectively introduced to the African Church.

There are those who would argue that preaching from the
Bible does not necessarily result in authentic biblical preaching. The answer would be that handling the text properly is
the second step in proclamation. At least the African preacher
is firmly established in the first step, namely, preaching from
the Bible. This does not mean we should not improve; by all
means, we should. However, those who take serious offense
concerning mishandling of the Bible should remember Paul's
warning to the Philippian church: "The important thing is
that in every way, whether from false motives or true, Christ is
preached. And because of this I rejoice" (1:18).

The main point is that biblical preaching is the only type
of proclamation that was introduced to the life of the church
in Africa. New congregations have flourished across the continent through this vivid type of preaching. Believers throughout Africa have patiently listened to the Word expounded
either in sanctuaries or in the shade of big trees. It is, therefore, necessary that preachers who rely on this one very
significant method of proclamation should seriously strive to
understand the Bible in order to interpret its message accu-
rately and rightly handle the word.

A story is told about a young woman who had heard people
talking about an interesting book that had just been published. She took the trouble to look for the book in bookshops
until she secured a copy for herself. After reading the introduction and the first chapter of the book, however, she put it
away. It did not seem interesting to her. A few months later,
the young woman was traveling in a foreign country. She met

a handsome young man, and she fell in love with him. To her pleasant surprise, the young man was the author of the book that she had bought and put away. Upon returning home, she looked for the book and started reading it from the introduction to the end. This time, it was the most interesting book she had ever read in her life.

The interest, joy, and satisfaction that come from reading the Bible have their source in the believer's intimate knowledge and experience of God as Father through the life, death, resurrection, and Lordship of Jesus Christ, and the ever-growing fellowship of the Holy Spirit. Hence, Jesus' warning to the Jews: "You diligently study the Scriptures because you think that by them you possess eternal life. These are the Scriptures that testify about me, yet you refuse to come to me to have life" (John 5:39, 40).

We study the Scriptures not only to admire the Bible as literature or to understand it merely for purposes of interpreting its meaning, important as those incentives may be. A believer's main purpose in studying the Bible diligently is that, through the illumination or teaching of the Holy Spirit, he or she will find life in Christ Jesus, the author of life. ·

Chapter 2

Preaching and Its
Historical Roots

In the African oral tradition of the Shona culture of Zimbabwe, there is a story that way back in time immemorial Musikavanhu (the Creator of people) had a message he wanted delivered to his people. He looked for a messenger and decided to send a chameleon.

The message Musikavanhu was sending to the people was that after they died, they would have a second chance to live. The chameleon went on his mission. Musikavanhu waited and waited for the chameleon to return with a report of the execution of his mission. Many days passed, but there was no sign of the chameleon. Musikavanhu grew impatient and sent a second messenger; this time it was a lizard. For unknown reasons, Musikavanhu's message had changed. Now the message was that when people died, there would be no second chance; they would die forever.

The lizard ran as fast as he could and got to the people before the chameleon delivered his message. So the lizard informed people of Musikavanhu's message. Shortly after the lizard departed, the chameleon arrived, but when the chameleon tried to proclaim his message, people ignored him and said that they had already received Musikavanhu's message for which they had been waiting so long.

Concepts of proclamation are inherently embedded in African culture; be it the delivery of the message, the urgency of proclamation, or preaching in general—it is all there. The story mentioned above richly informs us that the African people know that God has always had a message for his people; God has always relied on his messengers, and the messengers must treat delivery of the message as an urgent matter. We shall discuss some of these concepts in later chapters, but now we shall turn to the origin and development of preaching in the life of the church.

It is essential that we know the difference between the two terms, *preaching* and *homiletics*. There is a tendency to use the two interchangeably, although they are not actually synonymous. Preaching is the proclamation of God's Word as revealed to us; it is the act of proclaiming itself. Essentially, preaching is the recitation of the acts of God as revealed to humankind, regardless of the media God has chosen by which to reveal himself.

Homiletics comes from the word *homily* or *homilia*, a Greek word meaning a discourse or sermon. Yngve Brilioth, a Swedish theologian, tells us that the first use of the word *homilia* is "in Ignatius' letter to Polycarp as a description of the word spoken in the congregation; most exactly, it refers to an address of admonition."[1] The word *homiletics* means the art of preaching. It refers to the science or skills involved in proclamation.

Thus, the difference between the two terms is that while *preaching* refers to the *act* of proclamation of the gospel, *homiletics* is the *art* of proclamation of the gospel. This art of preaching involves the construction and delivery of the sermon. Hence what we study in the classroom in preparation for proclamation is homiletics; what we perform from the pulpit on a Sunday morning is preaching. One could say homiletics and preaching are the two sides of a coin. Although the terms are not synonymous, they belong together. No preacher or pastor would be interested in one without the other.

We shall now turn to the roots of preaching in the life of the church. It was Vernon L. Stanfield who wrote, "The science of homiletics had certain historical antecedents, i.e., Hebrew preaching and ancient rhetoric."[2]

1. Hebrew Preaching

Christian preaching has its roots in Hebrew preaching. As one reads the Old Testament, one comes across numerous spiritual discourses that were delivered by the leaders of Israel, the judges, priests, and prophets. There are discourses by Moses, Joshua, Amos, Hosea, Isaiah, Jeremiah, Ezekiel, and others. These addresses concern Yahweh's message to his people. That message was often related to God's acts in history: the call to Abraham, father of the nation of Israel (Gen. 12:2; Isa. 51:1-2); the deliverance of Israel from Egypt (Hos. 2:15; Amos 3:1-8; 9:7); and the many other acts that these leaders believed God had performed in the history of God's own people, Israel.

Since this book is on biblical preaching, it is important to note the developments in preaching at this stage. The early Old Testament preachers were primarily exhorters who took the opportunity to interpret the will of Yahweh as they understood it. They were not preachers of the Bible, for the Bible was not yet the authoritative word of God.[3] They discerned Yahweh's revelation through tradition, world events, meditation on their faith, nature, and the many other ways God chose to reveal himself to his people.

Further development of Hebrew preaching came with the beginning of the canonization of the Old Testament around 621 B.C., when the Deuteronomic code, which the king of Judah read to his people (2 Kings 23:1-3), was accepted as authoritative. As we shall see, by 400 B.C., the first six books of the Old Testament had been accepted as authoritative scripture for Israel. For the first time, a preacher of the Old Testament period had scriptures from which to expound the Word of God. When Ezra and Nehemiah returned to Jerusalem from the Babylonian exile during the fifth century B.C., they specifically referred to "the Book of the Law of Moses, which the LORD had commanded for Israel" (Neh. 8:1).

Prior to the canonization of the scriptures, another important tradition had developed in Israel, the tradition of prophecy. Moses was regarded as the greatest prophet and the only prophet "whom the LORD knew face to face" (Deut. 34:10). Nathan (2 Sam. 12), Elijah (1 Kings 17–21; 2 Kings 1–2), and Elisha (2 Kings 2–9) are among the early prophets—men who felt the call of God to become God's messengers to Israel.

Jerusalem had been known as the city of God and the place of worship (John 4:20). No wonder an exile replied to his tormentors, "How can we sing the songs of the LORD while in a foreign land?" (Ps. 137:4). Jerusalem was where God dwelt and where he was worshiped. That worship consisted of two components, namely, offering and teaching. By the time we come to the eighth through the sixth centuries B.C., the preaching aspect of worship at the temple in Jerusalem was taking on a stronger emphasis through the prophets. Isaiah spoke thus: "Listen to the law of our God, . . . I have more than enough of burnt offerings" (Isa. 1:10-11). Jeremiah is commanded to stand at the gate of the Lord's house and proclaim the message, "This is the temple of the LORD, the temple of the LORD, the temple of the LORD!" (Jer. 7:1-2). The temple in Jerusalem had become the focal center of worship and proclamation of God's message for Israel.

In addition to the beginning of canonization and the growth of the prophetic tradition, there was a third new development in relation to the public-worship practice of Israel, the emergence of the institution of the synagogue. The origin of the synagogue is unknown. Although it is generally recognized that the establishment of the synagogue as a universally accepted institution took place during the Babylonian exile, it is also recognized that the later Persian period provided the conditions required for the institution to flourish. Ezra and his successors, the scribes, were products of the Persian era.[4] "While sacrifice could be offered only in the Temple, the reading and interpretation of the O.T. and prayer could be carried on in synagogues even in Jerusalem itself."[5]

The synagogue, therefore, was primarily a place for the "reading of the Law." There may even have been a synagogue within the precincts of the temple in Jerusalem or several synagogues in the city outside the temple (as implied in Acts 6:9). Since the main activity of the synagogue was the interpretation of scriptures, it does not surprise us to learn that it was Jesus' custom on a sabbath day to go to a synagogue (Luke 4:16) and that when he visited the synagogue in Nazareth, after reading the scroll of the prophet Isaiah, he interpreted the passage he had just read (Luke 4:17-21). Paul followed the same approach in his missionary program (Acts 17:2; 18:7).

The biblical preaching of today clearly has its roots in the Jewish tradition, especially in the institution of the synagogue, which originated as the center for the reading and interpretation of the Old Testament.

2. Rhetorical Skills

Christian preaching also has roots in rhetorical communication skills. Rhetoric is as old as the human race itself; people have always sought effective and expressive ways of communicating their ideas.

The art of using words effectively is not a monopoly of one culture; it belongs to all cultures. Neither is it a monopoly of one discipline; it belongs to most disciplines. One only needs to attend an African communal court or a clan or family occasion where formal procedures are observed. The manner in which a case is presented demonstrates that the African people have their own special skills in making presentations. These presentations are characterized by special modes of speech, such as the use of idioms and proverbs, and by traditional ways of responding to the one making the presentation. All this shows the beauty and effectiveness of communicating with people within a given culture.

A dictionary definition of rhetoric is that it is "the art of using words effectively in speaking or writing."[6] Another definition of rhetoric is "the faculty of discovering in a particular case what are the available means of persuasion."[7]

I have often regarded as most interesting the presentation made by Tertullus when accusing Paul before Governor Felix. Tertullus began his speech by saying: "We have enjoyed a long period of peace under you, and your foresight has brought about reforms in this nation. Everywhere and in every way, most excellent Felix, we acknowledge this with profound gratitude. But . . ." (Acts 24:2-4). This is a good example of the type of rhetorical skill that we find in the scriptures. Tertullus was exploiting all the rhetorical skills he knew in order to persuade Felix to see Paul's situation from the Sanhedrin's point of view. Even the Bible has rhetoric.

The importance of rhetorical communication has been recognized for thousands of years; the "oldest essay ever discovered, written about 3,000 B.C., consists of advice on how to speak effectively."[8] The essay was addressed to Kagemni, the eldest son of the Pharaoh Huni.[9]

Vernon Stanfield points out that while preaching was developing in the Jewish communities, rhetorical theory was, at the same time, independently developing in the Greco-Roman world and in many other cultures. He goes on to inform us that in 465 B.C. Corax and his pupils first recorded what became known as the rhetorical principles. This subject of study developed its greatest effectiveness in Greco-Roman culture, culminating in the writings of Aristotle (384–322 B.C.)

and the Latin rhetoric of Cicero (106–43 B.C.) and Quintilian (A.D. 35–95).

Preachers of the gospel have not often wanted to make showy displays of their artistic ability from the pulpit. If anything, they have tried to suppress rhetorical skills so as to demonstrate the power and promptness of the Holy Spirit as the only motivator. Nevertheless, the Holy Spirit, who utilizes all the talents given to humankind by the Creator, has not excluded the use of the rhetorical skills that a preacher may have acquired. Paul at one point said to Christians in Corinth, "When I came to you, brothers, I did not come with eloquence or superior wisdom as I proclaimed to you the testimony about God" (1 Cor. 2:1); yet he is the same gospel proclaimer who poses some beautiful rhetorical questions in the same letter:

Where is the wise man? Where is the scholar? Where is the philosopher of this age? (1 Cor. 1:20)

The use of rhetoric in preaching became more pronounced as the gospel spread to the Gentile world. It happened that the gospel attracted persons who had already received rhetorical training, so it became natural for such converts to use the skills they had already acquired to advance the preaching of the gospel.

What first impressed Augustine in the preaching of Ambrose, the renowned preacher of Milan (A.D. 340–397), was the latter's expressive rhetoric. That ability to communicate the gospel led to the conversion of Augustine. Augustine (354–430) became not only an outstanding theologian but also a preacher of the gospel. He was a homiletician and became the first of the Fathers to write on the subject of homiletics. In his book *De Doctrina Christiana,* he tried to establish the relationship between rhetoric and preaching.[10] The era of Augustine was a difficult one for the church because of the many heresies that thrived then. Augustine attacked such heretical ideas effectively from the pulpit, while teaching what he believed to be the Christian position. Such a task required the ability to speak clearly and convincingly.

John Chrysostom (347–407), a notable biblical preacher of Antioch, was introduced to biblical scholarship by Diodore of Tarsas. The School of Antioch was known for an approach to biblical interpretation, which treated the Bible according to its natural meaning, unlike the Alexandrian approach to biblical interpretation, which was allegorical.[11] Equally important was the fact that Chrysostom also studied under a famous rhetorician, Libanius, who even wished Chrysostom could have succeeded him—if the Christians had not taken him.[12] Thus, in John Chrysostom, we see the effectiveness of using the two traditions (biblical and rhetorical) in preaching as early as the third century.

Once in a while, the African preacher ought to remind himself or herself of Aggrey of Africa. Aggrey was known as a great orator. He was born in what was then known as Gold Coast, in 1816, and was educated in the United States of America. Most of us did not see or hear him, but he seems to have been a man who had a gift—and his speeches and stories are colored with African imaginative power. Take, for instance, the story of the eagle which had lost its power to fly, or the conference of the great rivers of the world, with the river Nile deciding to go to Africa so that her waters would bring new life to the Sahara Desert. Or better yet, take part of the speech that he delivered in Indianapolis in 1923 to a white American audience. In this address, Aggrey identified himself fully with the African Americans:

> You took us to the wilderness and with our song and joy we helped you make the wilderness blossom as the rose. You took us to the rivers and we helped to bridge them. You took us to the mountains and we helped to tunnel them.
> Black man of Africa, is there any future for you?
> We answered, "Try us."
> "You have given brawn," you said. "Can you give blood?"
> We said, "Try us," and you tried us, thank God, and on

Christmas of 1770 on Boston Common the first blood in the Revolutionary War was spilled. We went on until Salem Poor did his part, and Pater Salem away out yonder answered, and John Freeman at Criswold also answered, and all through the line in New Orleans under General Jackson we did what we could.

But that was not enough. Then the war between the brothers of the North and the brothers of the South came. Black man, can you do anything?

We said, "Try us."

Abraham Lincoln called, and we said, "We are coming, Father Abraham, 100,000 strong."

And they gave us the flag. They said, "You may die but never surrender this flag," and one black sergeant said, "Master, I will bring back these colours in honour or report to God the reason." He did report to his God with his blood, but the colours were brought back.[13]

The speech is rich with African imagery, especially the humility and vividness that one finds in stories told about African animals. For example, when big animals like the elephant, hyena, and others failed to find water during a drought year, it was the tortoise who succeeded. Aggrey's story of the "Black man of Africa" is characterized by that same success in humility.

To summarize this chapter, preaching as we know it today is based on two pre-Christian traditions: namely, Hebrew preaching and Greco-Roman rhetorical skills. If our preaching is to be effective today, we must hold on to preaching God's revelation of himself through Christ Jesus, his Son. At the same time, we need to understand our culture, or the culture in which the preaching is carried out. Above all, we must be in a position to utilize the art of speaking effectively, so that the people to whom we preach the gospel will hear it clearly. As Paul pointed out, "Again, if the trumpet does not sound a clear call, who will get ready for battle?" (1 Cor. 14:8).

Chapter 3

The Making of the Bible

A fascinating thing about the Bible is the manner in which it came into existence. The entire Bible (66 books) was written over a period of more than 1,000 years. It was composed by many authors, some of whom shall never be known to us.

It may be that none of the authors of the books of the Bible held the view that their writings would be regarded as sacred scriptures. The biblical authors wrote what was meaningful to them and to their particular communities at different times in the history of the community of faith. Their faith was in God whom they perceived in the events of history and in creation, and their whole future was understood in the light of that faith in God. Often, the biblical writers used materials which had been handed down by tradition—materials preserved in folk tales, legendary stories, sayings, and other forms.

Today, when we buy a Bible, we should remember that we are really buying 66 books, written by many authors over a long period of time, most of whom never saw each other. As we turn to the Old Testament, we shall see that most of "the writings outside the prophets are anonymous."[1]

Yet such anonymous authors still had one thing in common. They reflected upon the activities of God in the history of humankind, in the creation, and in the natural world that surrounded them. These authors understood the meaning of life and their own destiny in the light of their relationship with God. That was the common witness shared by the biblical authors, and that is the testimony they share with the generations of the faithful that come after them.

1. The Old Testament

The Old Testament consists of assorted documents, which were composed over the period from about 1200 to 100 B.C.[2] Before the eighth century B.C., oral traditions were handed down from one generation to another by word of mouth; various other documentary records and compositions were also available and were used by writers of a later time.

C. H. Dodd goes on to say that the books of the Old Testament, as they have been passed on to us, were composed during the period starting with the great prophets Amos, Hosea, Micah, and First Isaiah.[3] The prophetic ministry of the above mentioned prophets was roughly between the period 750 to 700 B.C. This was the time when the power of Assyria reached its height, and the history of the kingdoms of Israel (in the north) and Judah (in the south) can only be understood in the light of international events that affected them. The fall of the kingdom of Israel to Assyria took place in 721 B.C. and that of the kingdom of Judah to Babylon in 587 B.C., a little over a century later. It was in that historical context that the seventh-century prophets, Zephaniah, Nahum, Habakkuk, and Jeremiah preached, as did the sixth-century prophets, Ezekiel, the Second Isaiah, Haggai, Zechariah, and others.

The message of those great prophets of God brought Israel to a new awareness of her relationship with God in history. It was the prophetic proclamation of the deliverance from Egypt

(Amos 3:1-2), the appeal to the faith of the Patriarchs (Isa. 51:2), and other impassioned pleas that led Israel to think seriously about its religious heritage. The prophets interpreted the events of Israel's history not merely as facts of the past but as evidence that all that happened in the nation's history was the result of God's acting in history.

These are glimpses of the Hebrew preaching message that the eighth-century prophets expounded to their people; that prophetic message enabled Israel to look back once more into her own history in order to understand her contemporary situation. It was also in that historical and prophetic period that the Old Testament books began to take written form.

In the African churches today, people are beginning to raise questions about how the Bible was written. Modern biblical research has challenged some traditional assumptions. For example, Moses was traditionally regarded as the sole author of the Pentateuch, the first five books of the Old Testament. Now many people realize that there is no way Moses could have written about his own death in Deuteronomy 34.

At this juncture, suffice it to say, every preacher should recognize the need to study how the Old Testament scriptures were written. For example, there is the Graf-Wellhausen documentary hypothesis, which argues that the Hexateuch (first six books of the Bible) has four sources. The four sources are: the J Document that takes its name from its use of the name Yahweh for God; the E Document that derives its name from its use of the name Elohim (translated simply "God" in KJV and RSV), especially in the pre-Moses sections; the book of Deuteronomy (D); and the Priestly Code (P).[4]

It is important for the African preacher to appreciate scholarly efforts to get behind the scriptures we inherited as communities of faith for the sake of enlightened discipleship.

Numerous religious writings were composed by the Hebrews for the Hebrews, but not all that was written made it into the canon of the Jewish Bible. The books that did make it did so primarily for religious reasons. The word "canon" comes from the Semitic word *kaneh* which means "reed" or "measure." It also means a rule "in the sense of a rule for living a straight life."[5] Hence, a canon becomes a rule by which decisions are made. As we shall see with the canon of the Bible, it simply means a list of books which have been widely accepted by people as having religious authority over them. Therefore, canonization means "the process by which sacred books are selected, imbued with authority, and thus set apart from other religious writings that are either heretical or simply of devotional value."[6]

It has already been pointed out that the Old Testament as we know it today is probably only a small part of the total volume of Hebrew literature that was written. There must have been a widespread circulation, both orally and in writing, of historical traditions, stories, prophetic oracles, and psalms during the period between 1200 B.C. and 600 B.C. Out of that immense volume of Hebrew literature, the canonization of the Old Testament was achieved.

The year 621 B.C. was the turning point and the watershed in terms of the canonization process in the history of the Hebrew people. Josiah, who was king of Judah 640–609 B.C., supported reforms, including the restoration of the long neglected temple. In the process of renovating the temple, the high priest, Hilkiah, "found the Book of the Law" (2 Kings 22:8). The book was first read to the king, and "When the king heard the words of the Book of the Law, he tore his robes" (2 Kings 22:11). Scholars think that that book may have been the book of Deuteronomy.

Barclay points out that someone who had been a prophet and priest during the dark days of Manasseh (687–642 B.C.) and Amon (642–640 B.C.), when it was impossible to speak out openly, hid the book in the temple, where it was later found in the year 621 B.C. King Josiah publicized the book by calling the elders of Judah and Jerusalem and reading the book to all the people (2 Kings 23:1-2). The king also "renewed the covenant in the presence of the LORD" (2 Kings 23:3).

That event was the beginning of the canonization of the Jewish Bible. The process continued, leading to the canonization of the Pentateuch around 400 B.C. The next books to be added to the existing scriptures were the books of the Prophets. These books, which were already circulating, were divided into two groups: the Former Prophets (Joshua, Judges, Samuel, and Kings) and the Latter Prophets (Isaiah, Jeremiah, Ezekiel, and the book of the Twelve, or Minor, Prophets). The Prophets were accepted as part of the scriptures, or as having religious authority over Israel, in about the year 200 B.C. The final stage of the creation of the Jewish Bible added the Writings (Ruth, Chronicles, Ezra-Nehemiah, Proverbs, Ecclesiastes, Song of Solomon, Lamentations, and Daniel). With these books, the canon of the Jewish Bible was closed. The official closure took place in the small Palestinian town of Jamnia when a rabbinic assembly was held in A.D. 90.

The reasons which led to the canonization of the Jewish Bible were complex. First, as Gottwald points out, Israel was then lacking a significant present and Judaism was beginning to live in its past.[7] The initial canonization of the Deuteronomic code, which was immediately followed by the destruction of Judah in 587 B.C. and the long Babylonian exile, began the search for something that would give Israel a sense of authority over its life as a people.

Second, the rise of apocalyptic literature during the exile (sixth and fifth centuries) had an impact on the Jewish biblical canon. The term "apocalypse" comes from the Greek word *apokalupsis,* which means "a revelation" or "disclosure." Apocalyptic literature sought to dislodge prophecy, as it emphasized special revelations. Supernatural knowledge of the future was the source of the apocalyptist's authority.[8]

Finally, the rise of Christian literature forced the canonization of the Jewish Bible to its closure. Most of the emerging Christian literature was apocalyptic in nature. Judaism renounced this type of literature; hence, the rabbinic assembly of A.D. 90 which approved the Jewish Bible canon. The canonical books became the scripture of the Jews—the Book which had religious authority over them.

2. The Apocrypha

We shall now turn to another collection of books known as the Apocrypha. The word "apocrypha" was first used by two Christian scholars, Cyril of Jerusalem (died 386) and Jerome (died 420), explicitly referring to the noncanonical books. Jerome especially held the view that the books found in the Greek and Latin Bibles but excluded from the Jewish biblical canon were to be put among the Apocrypha. Such books were recommended for private reading at home but not for reading in the church or for confirming the doctrines of the church.

"Apocrypha" comes from the Greek word *apokruphon,* meaning things that ought to be secret or hidden. It was applied, according to Barclay, to books which were "too difficult, too sacred or too holy for canon use." After the fall of Jerusalem to the Romans in A.D. 70, there was a widespread production of esoteric literature in Palestine, including Greek Gnostic writings and Jewish Christian apocalyptic works. That outbreak was followed by the outlawing of apocalyptic works in Judaism (as demonstrated by the rabbinic assembly held in Jamnia in A.D. 90).

After such developments, the meaning of the word "apocrypha" changed; it came to mean "spurious" or "heretical." It acquired that meaning because persons who had not been "initiated into the lore of this literature believed that these hidden books contained heretical teachings."[9] While some church leaders like Athanasius (died 373) and Rufinus (died 410) used "apocryphal" to mean heretical, for Jerome the term meant simply noncanonical.

Apocryphal literature may be classified into two categories: the Old Testament Apocrypha, consisting of 14 books (outstanding examples include I Maccabees and Ecclesiasticus) and the New Testament Apocrypha, made up of types of writing similar to those found in the New Testament, namely, gospels, acts literature, and apocalypses.[10]

Although the Jewish Bible was closed in A.D. 90, the Septuagint, which is the Greek translation of the Jewish scriptures (the translation carried out presumably in Alexandria) was not closed at the same time. Consequently, the Septuagint included the Apocrypha. The Old Testament Apocrypha reached the early Christians through the Septuagint,[11] and "it is noteworthy that the Septuagint was the Bible of the early church."[12] That was one of the reasons that the Palestinian Jews were opposed to Hellenistic evangelization by Christians; the latter used the Septuagint, which included the Apocrypha.

Although Jerome's attitude toward the apocryphal books was that they were noncanonical but not necessarily heretical, his translation of the Bible (the Vulgate) was carried out from the Hebrew version. However, its content and order were influenced by the Septuagint. Augustine, who had accepted the Apocrypha as canonical, distinguished in his later writings between the Hebrew canon and the "outside books," the name sometimes used for the Apocrypha.[13]

The Protestant reformers, who decided to emphasize the authority of the Scriptures in place of the authority of the Roman Catholic Church, had to deal with the issue of the Apocrypha. In accordance with the view of the German scholar Karlstadt, Luther put all the Old Testament apocryphal books together at the end of the Old Testament of his German Bible translation.[14] He maintained the title Apocrypha. For Luther, the noncanonical writings were not to be held equal to the canonical writings. Only the latter were sacred. This is the position that seems prevalent in Protestantism in general. Even the African vernacular Bibles, like the Shona Bible, now include the 14 Old Testament apocryphal books. This is a sign of openness and acceptance of the apocryphal literature for edification, without necessarily considering it equal to the biblical canon. In the Calvinistic tradition, the Apocrypha was rejected outright.

The Roman Catholic Bible continues to contain the Apocrypha. As if in reaction to the Protestant leaders' rejection of the Apocrypha, the Council of Trent (1546) reaffirmed recognition of all the books contained in the Vulgate as sacred and canonical. That position has remained so for the Roman Catholic Church to this day.

3. The New Testament

Like the Jewish Bible, the collection of early Christian writings we now regard as the scriptures of the Christian church was developed in a long and gradual process. Out of many Christian writings, the church finally came up with the 27 books that we call the New Testament. It was not until the end of the second century that these books received general acceptance by the church; not until the fifth century were these 27 books officially recognized by the church as canonical for the Christian faith.

First and above all was the fact of Jesus Christ. In Jesus, God had broken into the history of humankind in flesh and dwelt among humankind (John 1:14). To those Jewish New Testament Christians and the early church, Jesus was the Messiah. This alone was the focal point of the life of the Christian community. Jesus Christ became the very center of their faith and existence.

There is another factor that went along with the centrality of Christ, and that was the existence of the Jewish Bible. The understanding of the Jewish Bible by the Christian community took a new perspective. They looked at it in the light of the Christ-event, so that the scriptures had a new meaning altogether. The Christians saw all the promises of the Jewish Bible fulfilled in Jesus Christ; they alleged that Jesus Christ was the one to whom the scriptures had referred. Moule is right when he says that the early Christians never bothered with the question of who Jesus was but rather emphasized what "God had done in him and to him."

From Judaism, Christianity inherited a conviction that the Jewish biblical books were the very "oracles of God" (Rom. 3:2); and in them, as the Christians believed, God had spoken concerning his Son. Some of the Christians referred to the "ancient scriptures as the words of God himself," in their writings.[15] Consequently, the early Christians put the Jewish Bible in a place of great honor. As Harnack says, the Jewish Bible became a hindrance for decades to the creation of the New Testament "because the Old Testament in a very complete and masterly way was subjected to Christian interpretation, and so Christians already possessed in it a foundation document for that new thing which they had experienced."[16]

However, the Jewish Bible was important to the Christians only because of the Christ-event. If it were because of Christ, therefore, Christ was more authoritative than the scriptures themselves; and Moule points out again that

> the early Christians were conscious that the voice of inspired prophecy, long silent, had begun once more to be audible; and they therefore used both scripture and the memories and traditions of the words of Jesus with the creative freedom of the inspired.[17]

Coming to the process of canonization itself, we cannot help starting by acknowledging the role played by the Apostles. Jesus did not leave his church a written record of his life or ministry, but one thing we are aware of is that he left a great responsibility in the hands of the Twelve. He invited the Twelve to be with him during his earthly life. They had seen him hungry, thirsty, tired, and suffering during his earthly life; yet in spite of all that, they had also seen him seeking to do the will of his Father. From his baptism by John to the time of

35

his Ascension, the Apostles were supposed to have been with Jesus all the time (Acts 1:21, 22). That was why the Apostles in their writings could point out that they were witnesses of all these things (1 John 1:1, Acts 10:41, 1 Pet. 1:16).

The Twelve were eyewitnesses to Jesus' life, ministry, death, Resurrection, and Ascension (Luke 24:44-48): a fact which became crucially significant in the canonical process of the New Testament. Paul claims the same status, as indicated in the salutation of his letters to the churches, "Paul, a servant of Christ Jesus, called to be an apostle . . ." (Rom. 1:1; 1 Cor. 1:1; 2 Cor. 1:1; Gal. 1:1, to mention just a few). According to Luke, an apostle was one of the Twelve who had been chosen and sent by Christ Jesus (Luke 6:13), an eyewitness to Jesus' life from John's baptism to the time when Jesus ascended to heaven. Further, an apostle was a witness to what Christ taught about himself in relation to the Law of Moses, the Prophets, and the Psalms (Luke 24:27, 44).

Paul claims that Christ Jesus, having appeared to Peter, the Twelve, five hundred of the brothers, James, and all the apostles, "last of all he appeared to me also, as to one abnormally born" (1 Cor. 15:8). It was in that post-Easter revelation from Christ Jesus to Paul on the road to Damascus that Paul was called to be a witness of what he had seen of the Christ (Acts 26:16) and sent to both the Jews and the Gentiles (Acts 26:17). Thus, Paul, having become a witness to the revelation from Christ, like the Twelve, claimed he was an apostle of Jesus Christ—taught and sent not by man, but by Christ himself (Gal. 1:1).

No wonder Moule said that the apostles "constituted the earliest Christian 'canon' or measuring-rod, the standard by which the authenticity of the Church's message was to be gauged, for the duration of their lifetime."[18]

> The Christian community was in essence not "bookish"; it had been called into existence by a series of events well remembered; it lived under the continued personal guidance as it believed, of the central figure of those events; and the time

would not be long, so it imagined, before he would return to sight. Its authority was the Lord and the Apostles.[19]

Eventually, of course, came the time when all the apostles were gone and all the eyewitnesses no longer alive. From whom could Christians find authentic witness for what Jesus said and did? By this time, Christian literature was circulating in the communities; it was the beginning of the realization of the need for the canonicity of the Christian writings.

Suppose we follow the seven stages of the canonization, as proposed by Kurt Aland. His first stage would be from the time of Paul to John;[20] that is, roughly between the years 35 and 95. In this period, "the words of the Lord" (Acts 20:35) and the story of his ministry were for the first time committed to writing. It is during this period that Paul wrote his Letters, which began circulating locally and, of course, were passed on from one community to the other. At the same time, the stories about Jesus were also circulating orally. Probably the pronouncements, miracle stories, sayings, and parables were circulating either orally or in written form.

The second stage is a period that would stretch up to the year 150. If we ignore the overlap with the previous period, we could say this stage begins about 70. During this period, we begin to see the four Gospels emerging in their prominence. Among many other writings, the four Gospels began to take a special place by receiving acceptance in a good number of Christian communities. The Gospel of Mark was probably the first one to be written, but this does not necessarily mean it had the first acceptance; each Gospel could be more popular in one community than in another. Therefore, for quite a long time, these Gospels circulated independently, particularly in the areas for which they were originally intended.

Other gospel writings in circulation at this time were the Gospel of Truth, the Gospel of Thomas, the Gospel of Peter, and many others. The Christians of that time read some of these gospels, if they happened to encounter them. Moule quotes Aland's statement that some "inspired" teacher could still stand in the Christian assembly in the name of the Spirit and of some great apostolic leader and be accepted during that period. But as time went on, things changed, and more literary tests of authority were exercised.

The four Gospels individually began to gain acceptance by most of the Christian communities. They were read more often in Christian worship, and they gradually acquired the same status as the Jewish Bible. Among all the Christian writings, the Gospels first achieved this high recognition. Other gospel writings, other than the four, were gradually eliminated. An interesting case is the Gospel of Peter, which in Antioch was first approved by Serapion, bishop of that city, around 200; later, the bishop found that its Greek was odd and that there were some heretical additions, which led him to reverse his decision. Therefore, that gospel was discarded. Such was the process the church faced during that period.

Immediately following the Gospels in general acceptance were the Pauline Letters. There is no doubt that Paul's Letters were in circulation earlier than any other Christian writings. They were, in fact, the first Christian writings. The three Pastoral Letters (1 and 2 Timothy, and Titus) were ascribed to Paul, so that they would be accepted in Christian communities. The Acts of the Apostles took advantage of Luke, so that it was also quickly accepted.

The third stage, according to Aland, reaches up to the year 200. For our own convenience, we shall deal with the third and fourth stages together. This means extensive periods both before and after 200. At that stage the canon of the Gospels is completed. It is during this period that Irenaeus, who was bishop of Lyons (France), wrote (around 180):

> But it is not possible that the Gospels can be either more or fewer in number than they are. For, since there are four zones of the world in which we live and four principal winds, while the church has been scattered throughout all the world, and

the *pillar and ground* of the church is the gospel and the spirit of life; it is fitting that she should have four pillars.[21]

It is not his logic in which we are interested here; rather it is the fact that Irenaeus mentioned the selection and acceptance of the four Gospels by that time as scriptures.

The Pauline Letters were gaining the same standing. About 140, Marcion, a brilliant scholar, was expelled from the Roman Christian community. He left with a considerable number of followers, of course. It is considered that his most vigorous period was between the years 150 and 170. Marcion quietly made his own canon, which is said to have been two-fold: It was composed of the Gospel of Luke and ten Letters of Paul. Marcion's action had a tremendous effect on the church in connection with the canonization of the New Testament. As John Knox says, Marcion motivated the church to decide which books they were going to use in their worship. Knox went on to point out that part of the reason for the creation of the canon was to use it as "an instrument specifically forged to do battle with these second century schismatics."

The problem with Marcion was that he rejected the Jewish Bible completely. Because he claimed that Paul was the only true apostle, all the Pauline Letters were at the top of his canon. Because Luke was an associate of Paul, Marcion accepted the Gospel of Luke; the other Gospels had no room in his canon. He charged the Twelve with corrupting the doctrine of Christ. Marcion's father was reportedly a thoroughgoing Gnostic, so we could say that Marcion grew up in an atmosphere with very strong Gnostic teachings. John Knox also suggests that Marcion probably grew up in an area or community that regarded itself as following the tradition transmitted by Paul and that some of the churches founded by Paul were "in sharp distinction from and sometimes in real opposition to other communities."

About 170, Tatian, in his attempt to prepare a harmony of the Gospels, employed the four Gospels and no others. That, again, was an indication that in spite of Marcion's influence during that crucial period the four Gospels had acquired an indisputable standing in the church. The great leaders of that period, such as Irenaeus, Tertullian, and Clement of Alexandria, are said to have fully recognized the canonicity of the Gospels and the Letters of Paul. The reading of these books in worship services became the recognition of their canonical validity.

This brings us to the fifth stage. According to Aland, this period lasts into the beginning of the fourth century. Now at stake were the seven disputed books: namely, Hebrews, James, Jude, 2 Peter, 2 and 3 John, and Revelation. For a long time, the status of these books was debated. Some were accepted in one community but questioned by others and vice versa, and this went on for a long time. Probably the most accurate statement to make concerning these seven books at that particular stage is that generally speaking, they were accepted, though the status of 2 Peter and Revelation was still shaky.

The Muratorian Canon is a list of books of the New Testament with brief notes about their origin and authenticity. It was found in a manuscript written at Bobbio, Italy, in the eighth century but preserved in the Ambrosian Library at Milan and published by Ludovico Antonia Muratori in 1740. The Muratorian Canon seems to indicate that all 27 books that we have today in our New Testament were generally accepted by that time in the church as authentic scripture.[22] The problem was that there were additional letters attached to the 27 books: namely, the letters to the Laodiceans and the Alexandrians, which has been "forged in Paul's name to suit the heresy of Marcion, and several others."[23]

The two apocalypses, namely Revelation and 2 Peter, had finally been accepted, according to this account. Some of the Christian writings like the Shepherd of Hermas were recommended for private reading but not for public reading in the church.

To complete our summary of the process of canonization, we shall discuss stages six and seven together, for convenience' sake. These two stages began around the year 350 and extended to the beginning of the fifth century. During this period, a series of church councils attempted to bring the problem of the New Testament canon to an end. The first of these councils was the Synod of Laodicea, which met in the year 363. According to that synod, the canon was made up of the Old Testament scriptures and the following New Testament books: the four Gospels, Acts of the Apostles, the seven catholic Letters (James; 1 and 2 Peter; 1, 2, and 3 John; and Jude), and the fourteen Letters of Paul (including Hebrews). Only the Apocalypse (Revelation) is not mentioned. Aland says that "exactly the same enumeration is found in Cyril of Jerusalem (Cat. IV. 36) and Gregory of Nazianzus (of Zahn ii.1, 216f)." By this time, however, the Apocalypse was accepted in the Eastern church.

Generally speaking, by that stage, the New Testament canon was complete, but there were still loose ends. Nothing definite had been officially pronounced as yet by the church. The 27 books of our present New Testament were accepted, and probably those 27 were the only ones whose circulation was encouraged. That did not, however, necessarily stop circulation of the other books. Therefore, confusion still existed in many communities, and no doubt some communities were waiting for the church to come up with something that would settle the problem once and for all. The Laodicean Synod, which was an attempt to come up with an answer to the problem, was simply a local meeting attended by the local clergy, and as we have already noticed, they left out the Apocalypse.

The African bishop of Alexandria, Athanasius (295–373), sensing the seriousness of the confusion that Christian communities faced, in his customary Easter pastoral letter of 367, decided to deal with the issue of the New Testament books that were generally approved by the church for Christians to read. Thus, for the first time an episcopal leader listed the 27 books of the New Testament as we have them today.[24] That was a step forward toward the formalization of the New Testament canon.

The second church council to consider the canon was called at Carthage in 397. The importance of that council was that the African church, for the first time, spoke on the canon issue as one church. As a matter of fact, that was the first time for the church anywhere in the Roman Empire to speak as one church on that issue. The whole Roman province of North Africa was represented at the council under the leadership of Augustine. The Council of Carthage accepted as canonical the 27 books of the New Testament, as we have them now, and sought for the approval of Rome, which was not granted until the year 419.[25]

As with the canonization of the Jewish Bible, there were several reasons for the New Testament's canonization. First, Hunter points out that it was because of "the emergence of a host of Christian writings of dubious value and authority." The circumstances were such that the creation of the canon was inevitable. Second, Aland pointed out that the New Testament canon started when direct contact with the Lord or his eyewitnesses (the Apostles) was no longer possible. Third, there was the challenge of Gnosticism. Probably Gnosticism was all the more subtle in its influence on the Christian faith, because it was so often found right within the church itself. As John Knox pointed out, the New Testament was necessary for the church as a defense against not only Gnosticism but other heretical ideas that were common during the infancy of the Christian community.

Indeed, the creation of New Testament canon was necessary, and down through the centuries, the Christian church has been based upon the understanding of the 27 books that now constitute our New Testament.

This chapter has presented a summary of the process by which the Old and New Testaments were canonized, as well as a look at the attitude of the church down through the centuries concerning the Apocrypha. Preachers (both lay and ordained) would appreciate the Bible more if they had a good understanding of how it came into being. Indeed, such a background would make biblical proclamation more meaningful and intelligible.

There is no question about the diversity of the early church, but if there is anything, apart from Christ himself, that helped to create a sense of the unity of the church, it was the canonicity of the two Testaments. Up to this day, the church is called to a realization of its unity and mission because of its study of the 66 books that were finally agreed upon as authentic scripture for the Christian faith.

Chapter 4

The Authority of the Bible

T he way one uses the Bible is to a large degree determined by one's concept of the Bible. A more adequate conception of the Bible is essential, especially
for preachers, if the African church is to promote sound
biblical preaching within its communities. Dwight Stevenson had something to say about this point:

> Before you can preach from the Bible you should settle the
> question of the relation of scripture to the Word of God. To
> be fuzzy at this point is to confuse the preaching ministry from
> start to finish.[1]

It is essential for a preacher to understand what the Bible
is, how it came into being, where its authority lies, and why
we regard it as the Word of God. That knowledge should be
shared with all the people of the church. A preacher who
has a good grasp of the Bible is a preacher who would feel
free in any pulpit of Christendom.

In this chapter, we shall look at the Bible under three
subheadings: the Bible as a book of mystery, the Bible's
authority, and the Bible as the Word of God.

1. The Bible as a Book of Mystery

Many Christians in Africa today treat the Bible as a book of mystery (mystery in the sense of being unexplainable or unknown). They regard the Bible as the Word of God, and the word which God himself wrote, but the mystery comes when they are asked how God wrote the good book.

One unfortunate thing about Christians who surround the Bible with mystery is that they end up using the Bible as a fetish. In other words, the Bible becomes primarily associated with magical powers. Allow me to illustrate what is meant here by sharing some African beliefs. Africans all over the continent believe in the existence of God. In the African culture of Zimbabwe, several names are attributed to him: Mwari (God), Musikavanhu (Creator of People), Nyadenga (he who dwells above), and many others. The African people worshiped God even before the coming of Christianity, but they worshiped God through their ancestral spirits, the latter being believed to be in the realm where they are able to make contact with the Creator, even on behalf of the living.

Further, there is a belief in both good and evil spirits. The good spirits include ancestral spirits, through whom prayers of worship are directed to the Creator. They are the spirits who protect the living from illness and misfortune. They serve as guardian angels to the living. On the other hand, the evil spirits include those who died away from home or in unfavorable circumstances; they are filled with a spirit of revenge and a wish to hurt the living. Often such spirits are believed to wander all around, finding refuge in caves, trees, stones, pools, and many other places. Such evil spirits surface in the lives of the living as *mashawe*—demons.

Generally speaking, it is believed that a person who is possessed by a *shawe* will become sick. After the sufferer visits a *n'nga*—a medicine man/woman or a diviner—a prescription for a cure is made. Such patients may end up with a fetish or charm worn round the neck, arm, wrist, or waist. Such a fetish is meant to ward off anything that might be sent by evil spirits to attack the individual. Many of our people, including some Christians, are still involved in such beliefs and practices.

The reason why such beliefs and customary practices are being reviewed here is partly to lay a basis upon which to raise the question: Do African Christians at times use the Bible as a fetish? Is it not true that at times Christians use the Bible as if it has some intrinsic and magical powers? The author raises these questions, because time and again he has attended worship services where evil spirits were driven from people through prayer and the laying of a Bible over the head of the possessed, as the demon is charged to leave the victim. At times, the Bible is placed right in the face of the possessed. The idea is that there is some mysterious power in the Bible which a demon cannot endure.

The mystery surrounding the Bible continues to hover over the minds of many Christians. Admittedly, there *is* genuine mystery about the good book, but that kind of mystery is described by George Hendry in the following words:

> In the NT a mystery is a secret which has been, or is being, disclosed; but because it is a divine secret it remains mystery and does not become transparent to men. . . . In the Pauline terminology mystery is correlative with revelation. The substance of revelation is the mystery of the gospel (Eph. 6:19), or the mystery of God (Col. 2:2), the divine purpose which was kept hidden from former ages and has been made known in the fullness of the times through Christ (Rom. 16:25f., Eph. 1:9f.). For Paul *the* mystery relates to the inclusion of the Gentiles as well as the Jews in the divine purpose of salvation. (Rom. 16:26, Col. 1:27, Eph. 3:3-6)[2]

Genuine biblical preaching will help Christians open the Bible in order to follow the "mystery of the gospel" (Eph. 6:19)—"the power of God for the salvation of everyone who believes" (Rom. 1:16)—expelling all the fears represented by the fetishes or charms that many of our people still wear. Such preaching should assist believers to understand that the power of the Bible is in the One who speaks through it, rather than in the book itself, and that maybe one could sleep better by reading and meditating over the message of the Bible than by literally sleeping over the book. Yes, what a mysterious book, with a mysterious message!

2. The Authority of the Bible

The question is often raised: In what does the authority of the Bible lie? In our study of the canon of the Bible, we discovered how the scriptures emerged from the community of faith over a long period of time. The Old Testament came out of several Hebrew communities and the New Testament out of several Jewish and Gentile Christian communities.

The argument has been advanced that the Bible is authoritative because behind it is the authority of the church. After all, it was the church that decided which books to accept and which to reject. As a result of that process, the authority of the Bible is considered to have been derived from that of the church. While the argument may sound plausible, the fact remains, as Alan Richardson said, "In authorizing a canon of scripture, the church recognized an authority which it did not create," namely, the saving acts of God in history, as we shall see later.

Another view that is very common in the African church is that the authority of the Bible is based on the fact that the Bible was inspired by God. The favorite biblical quotation in support of this position is from one of Paul's letters to Timothy: "All scripture is inspired by God and profitable for teaching, for reproof, for correction, and for training in righteousness, that the man of God may be complete, equipped for every good work" (2 Tim. 3:16-17 RSV).

The point Paul was making to Timothy was that biblical inspiration came from God; it originated with God and no one else. The problem arises when one tries to understand how human channels were used by God to convey that divine inspiration. There are those who advocate "verbal inspiration of the Bible," a view that holds that God or the Holy Spirit dictated the words of the Bible and that the human authors did nothing but record what was being dictated. Prophets were simply mouthpieces of God: God speaking through them, while their own intellectual faculties remained passive. Such a view of inspiration would subsequently lead to the conclusion that because the Bible was dictated by God, it must necessarily be without error.

It is very important to note that the church has always believed in the inspiration of the Bible. Both Jews and early Christians believed that the Old Testament was "written under the special influence of the spirit of God and that it possessed, therefore, a peculiar authority for faith and practice."[3] It is the purpose of this chapter to define that "peculiar authority" claimed by the Bible. Harold DeWolf is helpful at this point:

> Before each part of the Bible was written there were such events in the experience of the writers as to induce the writing. Inspiration is to be attributed primarily to these experiences and only secondarily to the passages in which they found expression.[4]

For example, consider the experience that overwhelmed Zacchaeus, when Jesus looked up at him in the tree and said, "Zacchaeus, come down immediately. I must stay at your house today" (Luke 19:5). That was the experience that changed Zacchaeus' life forever. The authority of the scriptural passages which tell the story of Zacchaeus lies not in the pages of the Bible but in the experience itself—the experience of Zacchaeus with his Master.

The Bible has authority, because it is the record of God's encounters with God's people down through the generations: God's call to Abraham (Gen. 12:1), Moses and the burning bush (Exod. 3:14), Isaiah's commission (Isa. 6:9), Jesus and the Samaritan woman (John 4:29), and Paul's meeting with the risen Lord (Acts 9:5). That experience—when God breaks into one's life through the revelation of Christ and the power of the Spirit—continues to this day in the African church.

The author will never forget a story told by one African evangelist. Kuda and Rudado were brother and sister. Kuda, the brother, was older than Rudado. One Saturday afternoon, Kuda was playing with his slingshot. A cock which their father had just bought was moving about their yard. Kuda aimed at the cock with his slingshot, and shot it dead. Because he had not intended to kill it, he started panicking. Rudado, who had witnessed the event, proposed that the best way to protect Kuda from the wrath of their father was to conceal the incident. Immediately, they dug a hole and buried the dead cock.

It happened that two days later the father noticed the absence of the cock in the yard and started asking the children about it, but they did not reveal the truth. It also happened that the father brought some sweets for his children, five for Kuda and five for Rudado. As the brother and sister started enjoying their sweets, Rudado asked Kuda for two of his. As Kuda tried to refuse, she threatened to tell their father the truth about the disappearance of the cock. Kuda gave in by giving away his two sweets. Demands by Rudado continued for a number of days until Kuda was completely under the control of his younger sister. Frustrated by his enslavement to Rudado, Kuda eventually decided to tell their father the truth about the disappearance of the cock, for he could not endure the way his sister treated him.

Contrary to Kuda's expectations, the father was not angry. After Kuda told the truth, his father bought another cock and slaughtered it for a family celebration dinner, because Kuda had overcome his problem and had regained the freedom which he had surrendered to his younger sister by not telling the truth in the beginning.

This experience of gathering the courage to tell the truth, followed by the discovery of the father's unexpected willingness to forgive his son, even going to the extent of celebrating as a family, was such an overwhelming event for Kuda that it changed his life. Kuda realized the great love his father had for him, despite his own unfaithfulness and untruthfulness. Such is the love Jesus spoke of in the parable of the prodigal son (Luke 15:20). As Paul wrote to the church in Rome, "But God demonstrates his own love for us in this: While we were still sinners, Christ died for us" (Rom. 5:8). The authority of the Bible is based on the human experience of such divine love, and that experience is testified to by biblical and contemporary persons and communities of faith throughout the history of the church.

3. The Bible as the Word of God

It is not always clear what preachers really mean when they refer to the Bible as the Word of God. It is easy to preach from the Bible without involving oneself in genuine biblical preaching. In order to maintain, or move toward a more adequate concept of biblical preaching in the African church, preachers need a clearer understanding of the Bible as the Word of God. To move toward that goal, it is necessary to raise two questions.

First, what is the Word of God? The term "Word of God" has different meanings. It refers to various ways God makes himself known to humankind. God reveals himself in creation, history, and many other ways. The moments of God's self-manifestation in the history of humankind have been treasured by the community of faith as God's acts or saving activities. These acts of God have been known as God's way of speaking to humans—God's Word. The New Testament gives us a clue here, as Stanley Schneider points out:

> The Greek term which is translated "Word" is the term *logos.* Fundamental to the meaning of the Greek term is this—it means "that which reveals the inmost thoughts or feelings of

51

a being," or the "outward form by which inward thought is expressed."[5]

The point to remember here is that although God has revealed and does reveal himself in many ways, primarily the Word of God is known as a Person, and all other forms of his manifestation are secondary.[6] This would mean "Jesus Christ is the Word of God,"[7] for it is in the Person of Jesus that God has been fully revealed to humankind. No wonder the author of the Letter to the Hebrews wrote, "In the past God spoke to our forefathers through the prophets at many times and in various ways, but in these last days he has spoken to us by his Son" (Heb. 1:1-2). Therefore, in the strictest theological sense, the "Word of God" is Christ Jesus.

Second, what is the relationship of the Bible to the Word of God? Having established the fact that the Word of God in the strictest theological sense refers to Christ, we must now define the relation of the Bible to Christ. In what sense is the Bible also the Word of God? The Bible is not the Word of God because some people evoke demons by it or because God dictated its contents word by word. Rather, the Bible is the Word of God because it testifies to Christ. Richardson writes:

> The Bible is the authoritative historical witness to Christ. It is the testimony of those who actually saw and witnessed to the saving acts of God in history (Exod. 10:2; 12:26-27; 13:8, 14-15; Deut. 4:34-35; 6:20-23; Judg. 6:13; Ps. 44:1; I John 1:1-3). This is the significance both of the OT and of the NT. Both testaments witness to Christ: the OT contains the testimony of the prophets to the Christ who should come; the NT contains the witness of the apostles to the fact that Jesus of Nazareth is he.[8]

For the preacher of the Word, it is important to know that in the Bible we are able to meet the living Christ. As Stevenson says:

In our own way we may say that the Bible is the record, the witness, of men in times past to God's saving activity. As a record, however, the Bible is not a mere court record—it is a literary record which participates in the power of the events that it records. It has the capacity to elicit in the reader and the hearer the kind of response that Christ first drew forth from those who knew him in the flesh. Far from being a dead letter—that is, when read in faith by the light of God's present Spirit—the Bible is living and life-giving. It surges with contemporaneity. It makes Christ contemporary. It confronts us with the living God.[9]

Here we can summarize our understanding of biblical authority: The Word of God is Christ, and the Bible, both the Old Testament and the New Testament witnesses to the fact of Christ; thus, the Bible is the Word of God, and yet only secondarily, or in a derivative sense. To understand the Bible this way is to establish a solid foundation for sound biblical preaching. Since Christ is the Word of God, biblical preaching must seek to preach not the Bible but "Christ and him crucified" (1 Cor. 2:2). It is Christ who speaks to his people, and not the Bible, for the Bible is dead apart from Christ. The function of the Bible in preaching is its participation in testifying not only to the events of the past but also to the living Christ, who speaks through both the Bible and the preacher's proclamation. Thus, the authority of the Bible lies in the fact of the living Christ, to whose Lordship the faithful of biblical times and of today testify.

Chapter 5

Defining Biblical
Preaching

Proclamation of the Word in the life of the Church is
central to the pastor's activities, because God's mission
includes a message, a messenger, and God's people—
humankind. That message is most often the message of love
and invitation to God's people—people created in his image
for a life of reconciliation with him through his Son (Matt.
5:10, 22:8-9; 2 Cor. 5:18-19). That invitation is by God's grace,
for no one deserves such favor. The messenger of God is one
who is penitent—one with "a broken spirit; a broken and
contrite heart" before God (Ps. 51:17, Isa. 6:5, Acts 9:5). And
his people are those whom he sees daily on the continent of
Africa, "harassed and helpless, like sheep without a shepherd"
(Matt. 9:36). Most African pastors see these people every day
in the communal villages, in the congested urban centers, in
the refugee camps—they are found everywhere, afflicted by
poverty, disease, malnutrition, and all the social evils related
to poverty.

As we seek to define biblical preaching in this chapter, it is
essential that we visualize that context in which the biblical
drama takes place, namely, God's message, the messenger and
the people. Retaining that awareness puts the pastor in a
better position to appreciate the centrality of proclamation in

general, and of biblical preaching in particular, as a primary task of the Christian community.

In his or her parish work, the pastor is expected to give high priority to biblical study and sermon preparation. There is no way biblical preaching could thrive without persistent and disciplined study of the Bible. Furthermore, because the Bible is still the only book many Christians in Africa possess, there is a great need for emphasis on biblical preaching today. A pastor would do well to follow William Sangster's advice:

> If, of the various types of preaching that we have classified, the preacher were compelled to confine himself to one, it would be this [biblical preaching]. No classification of preaching comes nearer to universality. By preaching through the Bible, and applying it to modern life, the preacher could cover (either directly or by implication) nearly every human need.[1]

What Sangster is saying is not that we should choose biblical preaching to the complete exclusion of other methods but that biblical preaching meets more needs of the Christian community than any other type of preaching.

In the previous chapters, we established how the Old and New Testaments came into existence, where the authority of the Bible lies, and what we mean when we refer to the Bible as the Word of God. Now we turn to the meaning of biblical preaching.

In the Shona tradition we have a saying which goes like this: "Kugara nhaka kuwona dzevamwe." What it means is that if you are going to assume an inheritance, power, or responsibility, you must first observe how others did it. Although this book is on biblical preaching in the African context, the author has deliberately selected as his starting point three Western scholars who have written books on the subject of biblical preaching. These three are Donald Miller, John Knox, and Ronald Sleeth. We will bring in other scholars from time to time, but our main task in this chapter is to look at three definitions of biblical preaching by the above mentioned scholars, while at the same time relating what we learn from them to our African cultural, social, and religious situation.

Therefore, the procedure that we shall follow is to present each definition and lift from it points of emphasis regarding biblical preaching.

1. Donald Miller

Donald Miller's definition of biblical preaching is the following:

> Expository preaching is an act wherein the living truth of some portion of Holy Scripture, understood in the light of solid exegetical and historical study and made a living reality to the preacher by the Holy Spirit, comes alive to the hearer as he is confronted by God in Christ through the Holy Spirit in judgment and redemption.[2]

Miller discusses the meaning of biblical preaching by defining what traditionally has been known as expository preaching. It is important to note that Miller does not subscribe to the narrow concept of expository preaching, which stresses the length of passage to be handled and the detailed analysis of the passage, even to the point of verse-by-verse exegesis. A good example of this type of definition of expository preaching is that given by Clarence Roddy: "An expository sermon is one that involves the treatment of a Bible unit more than four verses long. A possible comparison is that the textual sermon is an expository treatment of a short passage while the expository sermon is a textual treatment of a long passage."[3]

Miller is opposed to this narrow understanding of expository preaching as well as to the distinction made between textual and expository preaching. To Miller, "all true preaching is expository preaching, . . . preaching which is not expository is not preaching."[4] Miller would agree with Stevenson, who writes:

Every scripture which serves as basis of a sermon is a text. It may be long or short. The distinction between textual and expository preaching, based on length alone, is artificial and should be abandoned. All biblical preaching is at one and the same time textual and expository; it is based upon a text which it expounds.

If we have been accustomed to the idea that textual and expository preaching are two different ways of doing biblical preaching, it is essential for us to pay attention to Miller and Stevenson at this particular point. Indeed, biblical preaching should be understood as both textual and expository.

In his definition, Miller brings up three interesting points that help us see what biblical preaching is all about. First, biblical preaching is an *act* with the goal of accomplishing something. In other words, preaching is not mere speaking. Generally, people are not attracted by mere beauty of speech. Rather, speech is usually functional and is judged by its content or aims.

Second, Miller notes, "The substance of preaching, drawn from the scriptures, is to be found by painstaking study in the light of the best available methods of historical and exegetical research."

This advice should be heeded by African preachers, for some of us grew up under a narrow type of biblical preaching associated primarily with the inspiration of the Holy Spirit and very little with exegetical study of the Scriptures. The problem with that kind of preaching is that it lacks the dimension of depth which is needed for the growing Christian communities in Africa today. If African national decisions are to be made in the light of the Christian faith, the pulpit must take exegetical study of the scriptures seriously. Otherwise, the results are disastrous, as Merrill Abbey explains:

Lacking a sense of commanding reality in the Bible as giving meaning and directive to their life, men draw their formative insights and compelling motives from contemporary culture.

Even within the church they seek conformity not to biblical teaching but to the patterns of society.[5]

How true the long-ago words of Hosea remain: "My people are destroyed from lack of knowledge" (Hos. 4:6). Let the preachers of the gospel open the Bible before people, and as Miller says, the whole process will be quickened by the living Spirit of God, who desires to speak once more through his ancient witness.

Third, Miller goes on to say that the end of preaching is that the "sermon situation should be transformed from a human encounter between the preacher and his congregation into a divine encounter between God and both the preacher and people." In other words, a preaching situation accomplishes its goal only as God takes over, when it is no longer the preacher but God encountering people. A Swiss theologian puts it well when he writes:

> Preaching is thus speech *by* God rather than speech *about* God. Certainly preaching also has for its aim to reveal God, to present Him to men; but when we preach, our role is not that of the impresario presenting a star to the crowd. We are not there to explain to men that God is eternal, that He knows all things and is capable of all things; that He loves us and wants us to love Him in return. We are there in order that, through our preaching, He may say these things Himself. . . . God is thus at work in our preaching (Phil. 2:13, I Thess. 2:13. . . . Preaching is an event in which God acts.[6]

This is preaching at its best. God alone must speak to his people: His voice alone must be heard by both the preacher and people. Yet he speaks through the words of the preacher. No wonder the author of the Second Letter to Timothy wrote:

> In a large house there are articles not only of gold and silver, but also of wood and clay; some are for noble purposes and some for ignoble. If a man cleanses himself from the latter, he

will be an instrument for noble purposes, made holy, useful to
the master and prepared to do any good work. (2 Tim. 2:20-21)

In summary, biblical preaching, for Miller, has three essential characteristics. It is an act that accomplishes something; it
is wrestling with the exegetical task of understanding the
scriptures; it is a divine encounter with humans, God speaking
to his people through the words of the preacher.

2. John Knox

John Knox's definition of biblical preaching is presented
in a fourfold form. Knox asks a vital question: "When is
preaching biblical?" He is aware of many preachers who may
pride themselves on preaching biblical sermons, but he punc-
tures such pride when he says that merely preaching from a
biblical text does not make a sermon biblical. This is a point
to which the church in Africa needs to pay more attention
than ever before. An outsider who visited Africa made a very
interesting observation about the African independent
churches: "The new churches are, on the whole, devoted to
Bible reading and Bible study; translations into local languages and dialects help give the Bible its immense prestige
as the Word of God."[7]

This comment could be made of the established denominations as well, although it is most strongly applicable to the
new churches, as mentioned above. Still the question remains:
Since preaching plays such a significant role in these
churches, how much of it is genuinely biblical preaching? The
church in Africa does not have to judge itself by Western
standards, but there is a sense in which we cannot escape what
is apparently universal. Therefore, we need to look at what
Knox perceives as the nature of biblical preaching:

Biblical preaching is preaching which remains close to the
characteristic and essential biblical ideas: the transcendence,

the holiness, the power and sovereignty, the love of God; his demand of ethical righteousness; his judgment upon sin; man's creaturehood, his plight as a sinner; his need of forgiveness and release; the meaning of Christ as the actual coming of God into our history with the help we need; the availability of reconciliation and redemption, of life, joy, and peace, in the new community of the Spirit which God created through Christ and into which we can enter upon the sole condition of penitence and faith.[8]

Knox's first point is that biblical ideas should not be approached merely as ideas or abstract concepts. To avoid abstractions in biblical preaching, Knox suggests that these ideas be handled in their biblical context. That is important to remember.

How often have you and I heard preaching on broad subjects, such as the love of God, the fatherhood of God, the brotherhood of men, and many others? As central as these subjects are to the Christian faith, and as biblically grounded as they are, when they are presented without using the biblical context, the sermon may be a thrill to the ear, but the Bible remains closed to the mind.

Biblical proclamation for today's Africa must strive to help those devoted believers understand the message of Christ— not only through the sermon (which could easily be forgotten by tomorrow) but also through the Bible. In other words, the biblical sermon must seek to open the Bible to the congregation. It must help throw light on those difficult passages that believers are wrestling with daily. Most of our Christians in Africa spend considerable time with the Bible. Because of the large areas that some of our pastors cover, these humble believers are only able to hear their preacher once in a while.

When the pastor finally arrives, suppose that he or she is thinking of preaching on the love of God. Let the pastor contemplate such great passages as the Father who gave his only Son (John 3:16), the father who kept the door open for his son to return home (Luke 15:11-38), and many other scriptures which deal with God's love. A preacher who handles the great and central subjects of the Christian faith in this manner will have at last discovered the secret of the pulpit—namely, that he or she is both a preacher and a teacher of the faith. How greatly our African congregations need this type of preaching in a day of rapid cultural and social changes, a day when many "independent" religious groups are thriving. Our Christians need to understand their faith—and they will if the pulpit takes the Bible seriously.

Second, Knox goes on to say that "biblical preaching is preaching which is continually concerned with the central biblical event, the event of Christ." He emphasizes this point: "The preacher is still, first of all, a preacher of the gospel. His message is thus primarily determined by an ancient event—the event centering in the death and resurrection of Jesus Christ. Only such preaching is biblical."[9]

Since Jesus Christ is the focus of biblical preaching, ideas should be treated only as they are related to the total life of Christ. James Stewart shares with us an incident of two men in conversation after they have been apart for many years. "Whatever we started off with our conversations, we soon made across country, somehow, to Jesus of Nazareth, to His death, and His resurrection, and His indwelling," said one of them. How true this is with biblical preaching! Ultimately, Christ is to be lifted up.

Knox's third point is that "biblical preaching is preaching which answers to and nourishes the essential life of the church." A preacher who respects preaching and takes it seriously will be amazed to see what preaching accomplishes in a Christian community. Donald Macleod writes:

> There is a sense in which preaching or the sermon represents the most creative act of the minister. The whole pastoral ministry of the preacher comes to focus on Sunday morning in the sermon. With the background of a week of pastoral counseling and service in which he has become sensitive to his people's failures, needs, and sins and social ills of the commu-

nity, the minister bears witness in his sermon to how the gospel works. He brings to reality that singular facet of Reformed worship described by William Nicholls as a miracle in which "God makes the word of man the Word of God."[10]

The people in the pew, like the preacher, have hopes, failures, frustrations, fears, and doubts, which could be met by preaching that is sensitive to these needs. This is one way that biblical preaching can be meaningful to the African church—preaching that seeks to expound the Word in the light of a situation confronting people. Knox sees this kind of preaching as an "ellipse moving about the two foci of the ancient event and the always new life of the spirit." He means that biblical preaching does not see only the message to be delivered; it must also seek to understand the need for that message. The preacher must raise the question: Why is this particular message needed in this situation? What is happening among the people to make such a message essential?

Therefore, biblical proclamation for today's Africa must seek to understand both the message and the changing situations that the African nations and communities are going through. Only that type of proclamation helps the Christian community face its social and personal issues in the light of the biblical truth that nourishes its life as a community.

Finally, for Knox, "biblical preaching will be preaching in which the event in a real sense is recurring." In other words, preaching is not merely reciting the old events: it is the Spirit who gives life so that as the preacher is engaged in the act of preaching, "in his inspired words the past event is happening again." We preach the living Christ. The historical facts about the life of Christ or the saving acts of God are important only as they reveal who Christ is or what God has done and is doing through the Son. It is always Christ who must be lifted up. He is the message of our proclamation.

Therefore, according to John Knox, biblical preaching is preaching that remains close to biblical ideas; focuses centrally on the event of Christ, nourishes the church, and brings about the recurrence of the Christ-event through the act of preaching.

3. Ronald Sleeth

Ronald Sleeth's definition of biblical preaching is the last definition of biblical preaching that we are going to examine:

> Biblical preaching is the proclamation of the kerygma (either explicitly or implicitly) through the exposition of specific scriptural material directed to contemporary life.[11]

The first main point in Sleeth's definition of biblical preaching is that a "biblical sermon should proclaim the kerygma, either explicitly or implicitly." He defines the kerygma as "the life, teachings, death, and resurrection of Jesus Christ." Therefore, every sermon must touch some aspect of the Christ-event. Henry Grady Davis, in dealing with the characteristics expected in a good sermon idea, says, "It must be one of the many facets of the gospel of Christ." That is the point with which biblical proclamation should wrestle. It may be helpful for preachers to ask themselves as they wrestle with a sermon idea or text: What facet of the gospel does this idea or text present to me and to my people? Or which aspect of the Christ-event is the idea revealing to me? A biblical sermon must always address some aspect of the saving acts of God—be it in the Old or New Testament.

The second point in Sleeth's development of his definition is that the biblical sermon should be "the exposition of *specific* scriptural material." Sleeth's conviction is that authentic biblical preaching must be inductive, proceeding from the text to the broader theme. Thus, he emphasizes that the preacher deals with specific scriptural material from which exposition is done. While Donald Miller undertakes the task of clarifying and expanding the definition of expository preaching Sleeth seems to be concerned with preachers who use texts "as mottoes and pretexts" without any attempt to examine the scriptural passage. In fact, this seems to be more of a problem in the American pulpit than in the African church, although many Christian communities in Africa originated with American missionaries and American seminaries have opened their doors to many international students. However, Sleeth's position is that the preacher must deal with specific scriptural material—a point we have already exhausted under Knox's definition. John C. Irwin, who wrote on the same problem over 40 years ago, had this to say:

> Is there any reason why a passage of Scripture cannot be treated with only such emphasis upon its historical setting as will illuminate its relevance for today? At any rate when a preacher occasionally does find a Bible incident or passage which illuminates our present situation, the people hear him gladly.[12]

The third point that Sleeth brings up in his definition "is that biblical preaching is directed to meeting the needs of contemporary life." Unless preaching speaks to the needs of people, it is nothing. "True biblical preaching can be scriptural only when it develops a message from its source that can be proclaimed to the people in a relevant way," says Sleeth. This is valuable advice for those who rejoice in expounding the meaning of the Scriptures without laboring to show what they say in relation to a contemporary situation.

In summary, biblical preaching, to Sleeth, means proclaiming the Christ-event or the kerygma, doing exposition of a specific passage, and addressing contemporary needs.

There seems to be a consensus in what Miller, Knox, and Sleeth define as biblical preaching. Although the three may not quite agree on every point, their differences are merely matters of varying emphases. Here is what we have discovered these three men to be saying about biblical preaching.

First, biblical preaching is the proclamation of Christ. On this point, we have found that when Miller says, "Preaching is not mere speaking; it is an act," his emphasis is on the act of proclamation. But when we turn to Knox's and Sleeth's definitions, the emphasis is on Christ, or "event of Christ" and "kerygma."

Second, biblical preaching is exposition of scriptures. While Miller and Sleeth are very specific on this point as essential to the task of biblical preaching (as already indicated in their definitions), Knox mentions it in passing when he says that in biblical preaching abstract ideas should be discussed only "in the concrete context of the church's tradition and life."

Third, biblical preaching must meet the contemporary needs. Miller does not dwell on contemporaneity as do the other two men, but when he speaks of preaching that accomplishes something, or is an act, he is obviously referring to contemporary life. In contrast, Knox and Sleeth discuss this point at length. One of the most memorable parts of Knox's book deals with this theme:

> The preacher is not repeating, over and over again, an ancient chronicle; he is bearing witness to the quality and significance of a new communal life in which God is making available to us a new health and salvation. His preaching is an ellipse moving about the two foci of the ancient event and the always new life of the Spirit. Since one can truly speak of the event only in the light of the continuing experience of the church and one can truly interpret the life of the church only in the light of the remembered event, the two foci tend to become a single center. But the true shape of preaching is an ellipse, not a circle, and the tension between the event and the spirit is as important as their mutuality. Preaching fails as often because both are too easily identified as because either is simply ignored. To hold the two elements together in their full integrity and distinctive force, but *to hold them together,* is the basic problem of preaching.[13]

Miller and Knox also discuss the profound significance of what happens in the process of preaching. Miller states that "in the process of preaching, the sermon situation should be transformed from a human encounter between the preacher and his congregation into a divine encounter between God and both preacher and people." John Knox says: "Biblical preaching will be preaching in which the event in a real sense is recurring. The God who acted in the events out of which the church arose acts afresh in the preacher's word."[14]

Chapter 6

Biblical Proclamation
in Our Cultural
Context

I t is important that the worldwide church develop a greater awareness of African peoples and cultures. There is an even greater need on the part of African preachers themselves to begin developing more balanced perspectives on the African experience. We must devote ourselves to reaching a deeper understanding of Africa's past, its present frustrations as it struggles to move forward, and its dream and visions for its future.

The people of the African continent are still under the grip of many ancient and destructive forces, including hunger, disease, illiteracy, and superstition, to mention only a few. At the same time, the people are increasingly coming under the grip of new forces, such as urbanization, industrialization, a monetary economic order, and many others.

As people move to urban centers seeking new homes, they find themselves caught between the two cultures: the traditional and the new. They are constantly deciding which traditional practices to lay aside and which new practices to adopt. If traditional ideas are not abandoned completely, they are modified for the new situation. Others who might have abandoned traditional practices, under the spell of a religious experience or conversion to the Christian faith, may go back when a crisis strikes. All of a sudden, one realizes that without the traditional rituals or ceremonies, one is not fully equipped to face a personal, marital, or family crisis.

In this situation, the preacher of the gospel needs to develop an appreciation of the culture of a people. Often the cultural changes that we see today take place on the surface, but what is deep in the subconscious is never forgotten, for it has a way of surfacing in times of crisis. If some people in Africa no longer seem to share the traditional concepts and practices because they have an education or have been Westernized, watch them when crisis comes. Furthermore, the so-called educated ones are in the minority. The majority of the people still live on the communal land and hold on to their traditional concepts and practices.

There is a sense in which the church in Africa has misled its own people. It has not given the expected leadership to its people—the African people who seek to live a new life in Christ in the context of their culture. In the first place, the church condemned African culture as unchristian; second, the African church has not taken adequate interest in studying African culture in order to give guidance to new converts. Every human culture has good and bad aspects. All people, Christian and non-Christian, know this. We must keep this caution in mind when studying any culture, African or non-African.

Deep-seated in Africa's past is the belief in God as the Creator and the One from whom comes all that we see on earth. At the same time, the African people, like everyone else, have dreams and hopes, fears and anxieties; they have experienced frustrations and failures, like the rest of humankind. In their religious life, Africans believe their ancestors are not dead but alive (the living-dead, as John Mbiti calls them), still playing a great part in the daily life of the living. Hence, a religious conception of the communion of saints that embraces both the living and the living-dead. If Christ is presented to the African through such familiar concepts, one would not be surprised to receive as a response: "Were not our hearts burning within us while he talked with us on the road and opened the Scriptures to us?" (Luke 24:32)

The African church has the opportunity to adopt two cultural traditions for the sake of effective biblical preaching in the life of the church: (1) the African conception of proclamation, (2) the proclamation of the biblical message.

1. The African Conception of Proclamation

Since the writing of this book is not based on wide research, there is no way I can speak definitively of the "African conception of proclamation" as such. I developed this concept in the course of pastoral and teaching experiences in Zimbabwe, so I will use examples from the Shona culture to illustrate my points.

We need to begin by raising a crucial question. If the proclamation of Christ, the Act of God, is to be equally regarded by the Church as an act on our part, how effectively can the church in Africa discharge that responsibility? Maybe we should begin by asking: What does proclamation mean to Africans in their traditional religious context or daily experience? And how important is this concept of proclamation? Does the word "proclamation" evoke the same meaning for the African as it does in the biblical context? The Shona word for proclamation is *kuparidza* (literal translation, to announce). In order to get the full meaning of the Shona word *kuparidza,* the hearer does not only depend upon the words used in the act of proclamation. The message is also proclaimed through visible symbols, as were the messages of the Old Testament prophets.

For example, the people of Zimbabwe witnessed several ethnic wars during the nineteenth century. To protect themselves, the Shona groups developed ways to spread the word quickly when the enemy was spotted. The common practice was to set a big fire on top of a hill or mountain. That drew the attention of all villages in the area, warning them that trouble was coming. People would then wait for full information in order to understand the nature of the trouble. Messengers would arrive soon to announce the direction from which the enemy was coming and other necessary particulars.

Another traditional practice still prevalent in some Shona villages is the use of the drum. In the village in which the author was born, the drum was used for dance songs as well as for announcing death. There was a special drum sound known as *shima.* The moment the sound of *shima* was heard, those walking would stand still; those in the fields would stop working and start wondering who had died. The drum was also used to inform people of an approaching enemy during the ethnic wars.

It is regrettable that the use of the drum to announce the death of a Christian was stopped by the church, as it was considered unchristian. Instead, a bell was adopted by most denominations and is still rung to this day. Unfortunately, the use of the bell at the church does not seem to proclaim or announce meaningfully to the whole community or village, as did the drum, which actually talked. However, since the drum is increasingly making its way back in the African Christian worship service today, we hope it will regain its rightful place in the life of the people. It certainly evokes a sense of proclamation in the African context.

Probably the concept of proclamation is clearer when we turn to another aspect of the life of the African people. Among the Shona, there is a *svikiro,* or medium, to whom an ethnic group or clan may turn for a word of advice or direction in times of crisis. If there was a question in the minds of people about the right successor to a chieftainship, a medium would have to be consulted. Or in the case of a drought, when all the crops were scorched in the heat of the tropical sun, people would consult the medium. Again, it is the *svikiro,* or medium, who must bring a word of comfort or judgment to the people. Usually, a *svikiro* does not say anything until possessed. This means that a *svikiro* does not always give answers immediately when approached with a question. If a *svikiro* asks for beer to be brewed, then everybody in the village knows that sometime during the period of drinking and dancing, he or she will speak on an issue of their concern. By the time the *svikiro* is possessed, there will be many people around waiting to hear the message. Usually, a *svikiro* is given a mat on which to sit, and there is another mat for the players of the *mbira* (an African musical instrument).

At the only occasion when an ethnic *svikiro* spoke among the people with whom I worked, I was amazed to see that there were more than 50 people present. Others arrived later. It was interesting to see that so many people were that eager to hear the answers to their problems from the *svikiro.*

A *svikiro* does not always speak the truth about the life situation of a people. As soon as a *svikiro* is about to make pronouncements on anything of concern to the villagers, elders are called. The elders must listen to what the *svikiro* says in order to judge if the message and sequence of events agree with the history or tradition of the people. The elders accept the message if they perceive it bears relevance to their life situation. Likewise, they have the right to reject a message and to declare a *svikiro* a false *svikiro.* How amazingly close Shona cultural practice here is to biblical practice, as Paul instructed the church in Corinth: "Two or three prophets should speak, and the others should weigh carefully what is said" (1 Cor. 14:29).

Today, in the life of the African church, both independent and mainstream churches, the congregation responds "Amen" to all that some preachers say when allegedly filled by the Holy Spirit. The people do not seem to feel a need to test what kind of spirit may have filled the preacher. (It could be merely the preacher's own spirit.) As John wrote to the early Christians: "Dear friends, do not believe every spirit, but test the spirits to see whether they are from God, because many false prophets have gone out into the world" (1 John 4:1). An African preacher from Zimbabwe who seeks to communicate that Christian message from Paul and John would do so more effectively if he or she were aware of the tradition of testing every medium who claimed to be possessed by the living-dead ancestors.

The point is that some cultural concepts enrich our understanding of the Christian faith, and the church in Africa today has a responsibility to study its culture in order to communicate the gospel effectively. To continue rejecting African culture will achieve nothing but the mutual alienation of our church and people. When the Shona people set fires to announce the approach of an enemy, that was a form of proclamation that saved many lives. Those who listened and believed the proclamation ran to places of hiding, while those who did not were often mercilessly destroyed by the enemy.

What an opportunity the African preacher has to exploit such a rich heritage for purposes of genuine proclamation of Christ Jesus! If the church would understand and appreciate the people's problems of fear, superstition, and ignorance without hastily denouncing traditional practices as the devil's work, Christ would effectively find his rightful place within the African community. Proclamation would become more meaningful, and that sense of urgency and expectancy would be meaningfully fulfilled by Christ himself.

Many African people are religious. As a matter of fact, there has recently been a resurgence of African traditional religion. In Zimbabwe, we have witnessed that phenomenon, especially after independence when our boys and girls claimed that the mediums Mbuya Nehanda and Sekuru Kaguvi protected them during the liberation struggle (1966–1980). More and more of our young couples today have consulted the *n'anga* (diviner or herbalist) for the problems they face both at home and at work. This is a field which needs research not only by social scientists and those who implement government policy but also by theologians and pastors. John Mbiti, a renowned scholar of African traditional religion, had this to say about the Africans' closeness to religion:

> He carries it [religion] to the fields where he is sowing seeds or harvesting a new crop; he takes it with him to the beer party or to attend a funeral ceremony; and if he is educated, he takes religion with him to the examination room at school or in the university; if he is a politician he takes it to the house of parliament.[1]

Biblical preaching in Africa must strive toward understanding the thought patterns, experiences and lifestyle of African traditional religion in order to communicate the gospel effectively.

2. Proclamation of the Biblical Message

We have already found that the concept of proclamation is a major point in the definitions of biblical preaching given by Miller, Knox, and Sleeth. It is essential to emphasize both the substance and the act of proclamation, because the two are like the two sides of a coin.

The substance of biblical preaching refers to the acts of God as they were witnessed, interpreted, and recorded in the Bible by communities of faith. While some people would see the movement of Abraham from Haran to Canaan (Gen. 12:1-7) as merely part of the migration pattern of the time, a person of faith would understand it as an act of God, who called and led Abraham to a new land. The Bible is full of such acts.

Two great biblical scholars, Ernest Wright and Reginald Fuller, have named what they consider "the central faith events" around which the whole Bible takes form, in other words, the central encounters with God as recorded in the Bible: the call of the fathers, the deliverance from slavery, and the Sinai Covenant, to mention the three from the Old Testament.[2] These were followed by the three New Testament central events: the life and teaching of Jesus, his death on the cross at the hands of the Romans, and his resurrection as head of the new community established in him, the church.[3]

Christian believers understand these central biblical events as the acts of God—the saving acts of God to the world. Since the entire Bible is to be interpreted and understood through these central events of faith, the Old Testament central events find their fulfillment in the New Testament central events (Acts 2:16; 3:18). In fact, the three New Testament central events are actually one event—the Christ-event.

In biblical preaching, one must never forget that the message is God-given. And only as one is sent can one preach. "And how can they preach unless they are sent?" (Rom. 10:15). God never sends someone without a message, and that message is what should be proclaimed. You may refer to sin, death, hell, and similar concepts in a sermon, but God's message as found in the Bible is righteousness, life, the Kingdom and love. How often have you and I sat through sermons which never demonstrated the love, mercy, and forgiveness of God, which is what most of us need Sunday after Sunday as we go to church!

When you study the proclamation of the biblical preachers, beginning with the prophets, you will notice that while they pointed out Israel's weaknesses, they also always reminded Israel about the great saving acts of God—acts Israel had experienced in its own history. Hosea says, "When Israel was a child, I loved him, and out of Egypt I called my son" (11:1). Or what can we say about the New Testament preachers, who all refer to the Christ-event as the fulfillment of the Law and the Prophets (Matt. 5:17)? The New Testament communities understood God's revelation as culminating in his Son, Jesus, whom they believed to be the Messiah. They perceived their faith as a responsibility to proclaim Christ to the whole world. Paul puts it beautifully when he writes to the Romans:

> I am not ashamed of the gospel, because it is the power of God for the salvation of everyone who believes: first for the Jew, then for the Gentile. For in the gospel a righteousness from God is revealed, a righteousness that is by faith from first to last, just as it is written: "The righteous will live by faith." (Rom. 1:16, 17)

While preparing a sermon, every preacher should ask himself or herself the following questions: What is the message of this particular text that I am dealing with? What is the good news about it, especially to the people for whom the sermon is intended? What aspect of the Christ-event or the gospel is presented here? If such questions are asked, the text will unveil the message, and that is the message to be proclaimed instead of what the preacher may personally want to say.

We also need to turn to the act of proclamation as the task of the Christian community. How seriously does the preacher take that task? There are three factors, among many, that need lifting up. The preacher needs to have personal conviction in what he or she proclaims. If one preaches the Christ who saves, the conviction emanates from the fact that the preacher has been saved. It follows that the preacher knows what it means to be lost and to be saved. It is like the testimony by the man who was blind from birth and after meeting Jesus declared: "I was blind but now I see" (John 9:25).

Furthermore, a messenger of the gospel must feel compelled to deliver the message with urgency, knowing that failing to do so means that people perish. I can imagine how quickly a Shona warrior or messenger would climb up the hill from which he was to announce to the surrounding villages the warning of an approaching enemy. It was a matter of life and death. Thus, one should use every God-given gift to deliver God's message urgently, effectively, and convincingly.

That is what biblical preaching should be, and that is what one ancient preacher, Jeremiah, struggled with: "But if I say, 'I will not mention him or speak any more in his name,' his word is in my heart like a fire, a fire shut up in my bones. I am weary of holding it in; indeed, I cannot" (Jer. 20:9). Paul cries out, "Woe to me if I do not preach the gospel!" (1 Cor. 9:16).

Another factor is that the preacher of the gospel must preach the good news of love. God's love to humankind is central to the Christian faith, and love should remain central in the message of every preacher. How easily preachers forget: "When we were still powerless, Christ died for the ungodly. . . . While we were still sinners, Christ died for us. . . . For if, when we were God's enemies, we were reconciled to him through the death of his Son, how much more, having been reconciled, shall we be saved through his life!" (Rom. 5:6-10).

At times, I have heard church members wondering if they had any business at the funeral of a non-Christian, or whether they should put on their church uniform at the burial ceremony of a non-Christian, or whether the pastor should lead the burial service for a non-Christian, if asked to do so by the bereaved family. The African preacher of the gospel needs to be reminded of the gospel of love: That "God is love" (1 John 4:16) and that long before we knew God, God loved us, will need to be proclaimed again and again. It was God's love which moved him to give his only Son (John 3:16) and to come and dwell among his people through his Son (John 1:14), despite the sinful condition in which he found all of us. What amazing grace! Love should guide the life of the Christian preacher; love should temper the tone and language of the preacher.

Finally, a preacher of the gospel should be one who presents himself or herself "to God as one approved" (2 Tim. 2:15). A faithful and conscientious preacher is bound to be concerned about a good worship service, well-ordered prayers, the reading of scripture, and well-prepared sermons. That is all well and good; it needs to be done. While John Knox agrees that a sermon, as an act of oral communication between the preacher and the congregation needs to be well prepared, he also points out: "But the aim of the preparation is clear; it is a man prepared, not a sermon prepared." If we spend that much time preparing a sermon, how much more time should we spend preparing ourselves, so that we are "made holy, useful to the Master and prepared to do any good work" (2 Tim. 2:21). That is what it takes to be a workman or workwoman approved by God.

Proclaiming the gospel in our cultural context requires that we recognize the fact that we reach people by knowing and understanding their culture. Culture is communication, and it cannot be ignored. That is why we have to understand some aspects of Hebrew and Greek culture in order to understand the biblical message. However, we must also recognize that the message to be proclaimed is not culture; it is the gospel, the Christ-event. As preachers proclaim Christ through thought-forms and conceptions that people will understand, they should never forget that personal experience, a life of love and constant dedication to God as one approved, also matters. The message of God often reaches God's people through his faithful messengers.

Chapter 7

Biblical Preaching
as a Method

B iblical preaching is not the only method of preaching. Two other common methods of preaching are topical and doctrinal preaching. In topical preaching, also known as life-situation preaching, the preacher discusses Christian themes from the Bible and/or from a life situation. It is very often associated with preaching on contemporary social problems. The sermon is introduced by a life situation—a contemporary life situation, which catches the interest and attention of the congregation. It is good for every preacher to present a topical sermon once in a while when such life situations call for it.

Equally common is doctrinal preaching. Doctrinal preaching is proclamation that begins with or rests on a doctrinal substructure. Doctrinal themes include temptation, sin, love, forgiveness, grace, atonement, reconciliation, and many others. Merrill Abbey is right when he says these themes are the "real power of pulpit evangelism." As doctrinal preaching develops these historic Christian teachings, the sermon becomes meaningful for both preacher and congregation. It is important for every preacher to preach doctrinal sermons to enable the congregation to understand the doctrines of the church.

However, the purpose of this chapter is to look at biblical preaching as the principal way of preaching the gospel; as William Sangster says, "Done well, it is perhaps the greatest service a preacher can render his people." Biblical preaching is the method of preaching in which every preacher should strive to excel. Biblical preaching encourages the study of the Bible by both the preacher and the congregation, and it equips God's people for service in the world (Eph. 4:12). Done well, biblical preaching always touches on doctrinal themes and topical life situations.

1. The Importance of Biblical Preaching

As we have discovered, a major aspect of biblical preaching is the exposition of scriptural material. Expository or exegetical research on a scriptural passage is a significant aspect of biblical preaching. Faithful exegetical study of a passage always helps the preacher to discover the proposition of that particular passage, which in turn often becomes the proposition of the sermon. A warning against the abuse of the text in preaching should be sounded here: A preacher should guard against "eisegesis." "Eisegesis is reading one's own ideas *into (eis)* a passage, whereas 'exegesis' is bringing *out (ex)* the real meaning of the passage."[1] The latter is what genuine biblical preaching is all about: to bring out the real meaning of the passage of scripture. It will take all kinds of tools to bring out that meaning. The preacher will need to use the original biblical language (if possible), commentaries, theological word-books, and other resources.

It is important to realize that the specific concept of expository preaching may be new to African preachers. Like many other African peoples, the Shona did not have written religious literature. Consequently, the question is: Can a people whose background is so bare, as far as literature is concerned, feel at home with expository preaching? Of course, they can learn to adopt the new methodology. The African has learned to adopt many things through the various periods of rapid social and cultural change. However, this does not mean ignoring our African heritage. The fact that many African people do not have traditional sacred scriptures does not imply emptiness in their heritage.

One of the greatest gifts the African people have is their ability to communicate orally. One only needs to listen to an African elder telling a story to children or a group of people. Or better still, one ought to listen to a village man presenting a case before the chief's council, without even a piece of paper in his hand. What a moving presentation! African preachers have plenty of untapped resources insofar as the art of effective delivery is concerned. We do not have to be European or American in an African pulpit. Professional training in the delivery of a sermon should help us to rediscover the talents and skills available in our own culture. How right the African American preacher Henry H. Mitchell, is: "The fact is that all too many Black preachers never managed to combine the gifts of a Black raconteur with the skills and professional training of a bachelor of divinity."[2]

So far, there seems to have been more adoption of African ideas by independent churches than by the established ones. There is considerable truth in the following statement regarding the matter of traditional culture in Africa:

> There are also cultural factors, ranging from painful decisions churches must make over customary practices, to tensions, suspicions and problems within the new society. This is going to create even more trouble because while Africa is becoming more interested in its cultural heritage, the old churches are hardly stirring to find a new approach to traditional Africa.[3]

The older churches may have to learn from the younger independent churches on this issue. The Apostolic Church of Johanne Maranke, an independent church that broke off from the Methodist (now United Methodist) Church in Zimbabwe in 1932, is a fascinating church in its preaching style. The preacher is always "accompanied by a Bible reader, who reads pre-selected verses from time to time on a signal from the preacher to illustrate and punctuate the message."[4] The preacher does not use a manuscript; instead, he delivers exhortations on the biblical text that is read. The congregation follows the reader, since they all bring their Bibles with them. The preacher holds a staff in his hand.

African preachers from mainstream churches need to observe some of these brethren more closely than has been done in the past. The independent churches may have something to offer to the rest of the church in Africa at a time when most African preachers seem burdened with foreign ideas in the pulpit. This kind of adoption of African traditions may make biblical proclamation for today's Africa more meaningful and more effective. Better expository methods in dealing with scriptures are urgently needed. We have often heard and read that the Bible is the most widely sold and most poorly read book. Others have gone to the extent of saying it is the least read book. Nevertheless, we want to believe that the churches in Africa, old and young, are devoted to the reading of the Bible; African preachers must build biblical proclamation on that firm foundation.

2. Various Types of Expository Preaching

There are various ways of doing expository preaching. First, there is textual preaching. We have already noted Dwight Stevenson's proposition that all biblical preaching is at one and the same time textual and expository. In agreement with Stevenson, the author, therefore, regards textual preaching as part of expository preaching or as a way of executing expository preaching.

When preparing an expository sermon, we should remind ourselves that the Bible was not originally divided into numbered chapters and verses. The books of the Bible were first divided into chapters by Stephen Langton, the archbishop of Canterbury, in the thirteenth century. In 1550, a French printer named Robert Etienne divided the Greek New Testament into 7,959 verses. The Geneva Bible of 1560 did the same for the Old Testament and Apocrypha. The purpose of this system of numbering was to make the Bible easier to study.[5]

While an expository sermon would normally deal with more than a single biblical verse, a textual sermon, by contrast, would normally be restricted to a single verse or short text. The distinction may not be precise, because a textual sermon could very easily be based on more than one biblical verse, and vice versa. Therefore, the distinction is only for purposes of convenience.

There are several ways in which a text or verse is used in preaching. We shall look at three of these. Often there are texts that divide themselves easily into a sermon outline. For example: "First go and be reconciled to your brother; then come and offer your gift" (Matt. 5:24). The sermon outline could be a two-point sermon:

I.   "First go and be reconciled to your brother."
II. "Then come and offer your gift."

Another approach to textual preaching uses a biblical text as the starting point for a sermon. The sermon would be faithful to the text. The sermon outline would be guided by the content and spirit of the text under consideration. We could take the following text as an example of this approach: "The word of God came to John son of Zechariah in the desert" (Luke 3:2). The sermon outline could be:

I.   John was a wilderness prophet.
II. John received a message from God.

The third method of textual preaching (which the author observed in Europe) used the entire verse under consideration as a repeated subpoint in a sermon outline. For example, John 13:36 would be outlined as follows:

 I.   "Where I am going, you cannot follow now, but you will follow later."

 This section of the sermon would deal with where Jesus was going then.

 II.   "Where I am going, you cannot follow now, but you will follow later."

 This section of the sermon would deal with the reasons why the disciples could not follow Jesus immediately.

 III.   "Where I am going, you cannot follow now, but you will follow later."

 This section of the sermon would deal with the reason why the disciples would be able to follow Jesus later.

Each section would discuss a part of the text, but the whole text or verse would serve as a repeated subpoint of the sermon.

Textual preaching can also be done from a longer text or multiple texts. This type of sermon might be based on a section of a chapter, a complete chapter, more than one chapter, or a complete book of the Bible. In theory, one could even preach a sermon on the whole Bible. Whatever choice of text a preacher makes, the principle of textual preaching remains the same: faithfulness to the context and spirit of the text.

Some texts lend themselves easily to such treatment in preaching. The parables, narratives, miracle stories, and many others suggest themselves immediately. This approach to preaching has the double advantage of enabling the preacher to study the Scriptures diligently and, at the same time, encouraging the congregation to read the Bible with greater understanding. Whatever approach a preacher may use, whether a textual or multiple-verses approach, expository preaching plays a significant role in equipping a congregation with a deeper understanding of the Bible and the Christian faith.

3. The Interpretation of a Specific Passage

Interpretation of the Bible requires skills, and those skills have to be acquired. Any preacher who has graduated from a recognized theological college is supposed to have acquired the skills and some of the tools needed for faithful handling and interpretation of the Scriptures. A preacher who seeks to excel in biblical preaching must remember several basic rules. First, there is the examination of the text itself. A preacher needs to acquaint himself or herself with the history of biblical text and its transmission. The literary style reflected in the text is also important.

As Harrell Beck informs us, the Old Testament literature is a collection which includes the following types of material: "songs and stories, historical narratives, codes of law, prophetic oracles (God communicating with man), hymns and prayers (man communicating with God), and wisdom writings (both practical proverbs) and speculative (Job and Ecclesiastes)."[6] The Gospels are believed to be based on five basic forms of oral tradition through which the Christian faith was transmitted: (1) pronouncement stories, or brief narratives meant to describe encounters between Jesus and people; (2) miracle stories of Jesus; (3) sayings of Jesus which originally circulated independently; (4) parables characteristic of Jesus' words; and (5) stories about Jesus, such as that of the Transfiguration. A little background on the type of biblical text under consideration and the history of its transmission from oral to written form increases our appreciation of the faithfulness of past generations of Christians to the gospel.

The preacher would also have to determine the historical situation of the text. Here several questions come to mind: Who wrote the text? Where did he write from? Who were the first people to read the message? Why was the text written? What is the message of the text? For a preacher to find answers to the above questions, he or she would have to use research tools: the original language in which the text was written, commentaries, theological word-books, and many others. Such books help the preacher to understand the message in the light of its context and the background from which it emerged.

In the Shona language, we have a saying, "Zvipukutu zvi-nogashidzana mhute." (The literal meaning is that hills situated side by side hand each other fog.) Our Bible consists of the Old and the New Covenants. One cannot preach from one without referring to the other. When one preaches from the Old Testament, it is important to recognize the Old Testament in its own right and to expound the revelation as Israel experienced it. However, the passage must also be understood in the light of God's revelation through Christ, which makes it necessary to bring in the New Testament. The reverse is equally true. As one labors to interpret a New Testament passage, it is often only when one goes back to the Old Testament that the significance of the New Testament passage becomes clear.

It is absolutely essential that a preacher of the Word be familiar with both the Old and New Testaments and make use of both in proclaiming the Word. Indeed, as two hills share fog, so do the two covenants witness to the same God who spoke in the past through the prophets and in the present through the Son, Christ Jesus (Heb. 1:1-2).

Let it be emphasized once more that we do not preach the Bible; rather the preacher is called to preach Christ crucified (1 Cor. 2:2). A study of the Bible clearly reveals that the Scriptures bear witness to the faithful communities and persons who witnessed the activities of God in many ways, including the Christ-event, in which God "made his dwelling among us" (John 1:14).

The New Testament plays a unique role in the preaching and interpretation of God's revelation to humankind. In discussing the history of salvation, Oscar Cullmann points out that it includes the past, present, and future. The center of that history is "the period of direct revelation, or the period of the incarnation." Cullmann defines the period of incarnation as extending from the birth of Christ to the death of the last apostle.[7] The testimony of eyewitnesses to the Christ-event is what we have in the pages of the New Testament.

Because the Scriptures bear unique witness to the Christ-event, the Bible plays a vital role in proclamation. The Bible actually participates in the proclamation of Christ, because it constitutes the unique witness of faithful communities to Christ.

4. Expository Preaching for Africa Today

Now let us raise a central question: How significant is the exposition of the Scriptures in Africa today? To this question, four responses must be provided. First, expository preaching in Africa today could be like a good seed falling on good, fertile soil, destined to yield "a hundred times" (Mark 4:8). I say *fertile* soil because of the great desire among those who have become Christian to study the Bible. People crave to know more about their new faith. This is the reason why many adults go to literacy classes. They are like the Ethiopian man who replied to Philip's asking whether he understood what he read: " 'How can I,' he said, 'unless someone explains it to me?' " (Acts 8:31).

These new Christians are reading and studying, but unless someone who understands the interpretation of the Bible helps them, the Bible will remain closed. And worse still, many will continue using it as a fetish. This situation can be ad-

dressed more adequately if the church in Africa today emphasizes biblical preaching. The author also recognizes the opportunity for witnessing to the fullness of Christ. What an
opportunity to give African congregations the answer to the
question asked by that African from Ethiopia: "Tell me,
please, who is the prophet talking about, himself or someone
else?" (Acts 8:34).

Second, expository preaching will familiarize Christians in
Africa with the teachings of the church's faith. With many
sectarian groups arising in southern Africa particularly, very
often Christians are challenged to rethink what they believe.
A good number of our Christians have moved from one sect
to another or from an established denomination to some new
sect, partly because they are not sure what their church believes or teaches. Therefore, here is another need that must
be met in a number of our Christian communities.

Third, expository preaching truly nourishes the church.
People meet baffling problems at home, at work, and in many
other situations. Most of them may not have the opportunity
to reflect upon the Word of God until they come to church.
Very often a sermon based on a specific scriptural passage,
which not only exegetes that text but also proclaims Christ as
Lord and Savior, answers someone's "hang-ups"; it may also
force the parishioner to go and study that particular passage
again at home.

Fourth, biblical preaching equips the church for God's
mission and service in its community. Probably no one is more
convincing here than Wallace E. Fisher who writes passion-
ately on the subject:

> Apart from biblical preaching, worship becomes esoteric or
> perfunctory; the sacraments are viewed as cultic rites or me-
> chanical tests for membership; evangelism remains a human
> activity; stewardship is equated with "raising the budget." The
> neglect of biblical preaching weakens the church's witness
> because it violates the biblical image of ministry.[8]

There has been great emphasis on lay training in Africa. The laity have been trained for leadership in the church as an institution, for special ministries, such as urban ministry, and for participation in other institutions, including government. The problem comes when one raises the question: Where should lay training take place? In a report of the consultation for South, East, and Central Africa on the training of the laity, one of the main objectives was defined:

> To take an active and intelligent part in the worship of the church, to practice personal prayer, worship and Bible study, and to develop habits of study and reflection regarding the Christian faith and the world in which one lives.[9]

This kind of training cannot be assigned to special training centers alone. Training must begin in the local churches, and this can only happen if biblical preachers recognize the tremendous role they must play in helping the local churches to understand themselves fully as communities of God which exist to participate in the mission of God in the world. Indeed, Miller has an appropriate message for the African preacher: "All true preaching is expository preaching, and preaching which is not expository is not preaching."

Chapter 8

Biblical Preaching
and the Lectionary

It happens often that a preacher is gripped by a message which he or she feels must be preached. That feeling could come in the form of a biblical text, a life-situation experience, or simply an idea. Any preacher with experience knows that while there are days of plenty when sermon ideas come easily, there are also days of drought when a preacher may wonder as late as Saturday evening what the sermon for Sunday morning will be.

The ideal situation would be to live in days of abundance all the time, and that could be achieved to a considerable degree by planning biblical preaching in conjunction with the use of a lectionary. Although there is no one lectionary for all churches, most churches agree on the division of the Christian year into seven seasons.

When using a lectionary, one learns that each season has a special emphasis or facet of the gospel of Christ. Most denominations have a worshipbook which includes a lectionary. The use of a lectionary helps a preacher to preach the wholeness of the gospel of Christ. It helps the preacher to avoid the temptation to preach simply from favorite books and texts and encourages a preacher to study the whole Bible diligently. We shall now review the seven seasons of the Christian year, which are Advent, Christmastide, Epiphany, Lent, Eastertide, Pentecost and Kingdomtide.

1. Advent

The word "advent" is from the Latin word, *adventus;* it means a coming or arrival. For Christians, Advent marks the coming of Jesus. Since the middle of the sixth century, "Advent has marked the beginning of the church year and is the first season of the Christian calendar."[1]

The season of Advent consists of the four Sundays before Christmas; it is the season during which Christians in their worship concentrate on preparing themselves for the coming of Christ. The meaning of the coming of Christ is twofold. There is the first coming of Christ, or the incarnation. Biblical preaching for this period would concentrate on those narratives which deal with the announcement of the coming of Jesus in the Gospels: the annunciation to Joseph (Matt. 1:18-25), the promise of the Baptist's birth (Luke 1:5-25), the annunciation to the blessed Virgin (Luke 1:26-38), the visitation (Luke 1:39-56), the birth of the Baptist (Luke 1:57-80), and many other scriptures in the Old Testament and the Epistles.

The gospel concerning the incarnate Word is primarily the news that God has visited humankind, "being made in human likeness" (Phil. 2:7). In other words, God, in Jesus of Nazareth, broke into the stream of human history and pitched his tent in our town or village as a neighbor (John 1:14). In the Shona culture, the incarnate Word has become "the ancestral spirit in front, behind and on the side" of the traveler. Thus, the thrust of the incarnate-word message is that "Musikavanhu" (the Creator of people) had so much love for humankind that through his only Son, Jesus Christ, he came to this earth, so that we would no longer live, travel, or walk alone. How vividly the Old Testament proclaimers shared that imagery of the incarnate Word when they wrote, "Enoch walked with God" (Gen. 5:22, 25) and "Noah . . . walked with God" (Gen. 6:9).

However, there is also the Second Coming of Christ. The New Testament Greek word which is commonly used in relation to the "coming again" of Christ Jesus to the earth is *parousia*. It means both "coming" and "presence." Van Harvey points out:

> The two meanings of the word, however, are still reflected in two somewhat differing interpretations of the second coming of Christ that have competed with one another throughout the course of Christian history. One interpretation stresses the visible coming of Christ that will bring a world full of evil to an end and will establish a reign of peace and order. . . . The second interpretation stresses the presence of Christ in the CHURCH, after the reign of which the world and its history will be brought to a close.[2]

While the New Testament as a whole seems to take the first view, the Gospel of John takes the second view. Harvey goes on to point out that influential early Christian writers, including Origen (185–245) and Augustine (354–430), favored the second perspective "of Christ's continual coming in the church."[3]

The Second Coming of Christ is a favorite doctrine of the church in Africa but also the most misunderstood by many church members. This doctrine presents great opportunities for biblical preaching, starting with Jesus' own message, "The kingdom of God is near" (Mark 1:15). There are apocalyptic passages which indicate that "some who are standing here" will still be living when the kingdom arrives (Mark 9:1, 13:30; Matt. 10:23), as well as scriptures that deal with the life of believers after death (Luke 23:43; Rom. 8:11; 1 Thess. 5:10; Phil. 1:23; 2 Cor. 5:8; Rev. 6:10) and the future glory when the whole creation which has been groaning since Adam's fall, waiting to be liberated, is finally redeemed (Rom. 8:18-25) so that God's work that was begun by the Christ Incarnate will be completed in the Christ Triumphant. Christ will hand over "the kingdom to God the Father after he has destroyed all dominion, authority and power. For he must reign until he has put all his enemies under his feet" (1 Cor. 15:24, 25).

The African church needs biblical preaching as a guide in understanding both the first and Second Coming of Christ. Advent offers every preacher a period of four Sundays each year to preach the gospel of his coming.

2. Christmastide

This season is brief; it consists only of one or two Sundays. The outstanding texts for the occasion include the birth of Christ (Matt. 1:18-25, Luke 2:1-7), the visit of the Wise Men from the East (Matt. 2:1-12), the coming of the shepherds (Luke 2:8-20), the flight into Egypt (Matt. 2:13-15), the Son's superiority over angels (Heb. 1:1-12), the servant of the Lord (Isa. 42:1-9), and many others.

The church's preaching and teaching about the meaning of the Christmas-event need to be improved. For example, many Christians still believe that Jesus of Nazareth was born on December 25. Biblical preachers should teach believers how the date of December 25 was adopted by the church to celebrate the birth of Jesus. Not until the fourth century did the celebration of the festival on December 25 begin to spread from Rome to the other churches. Most likely, the majority of early Christians did not know anything about the festival of Christmas.

One of the greatest early sermons about the Christmas festival was preached by John Chrysostom of Antioch on December 20, 386. In that sermon, Chrysostom urged his congregation to attend worship on the 25th, so that they could celebrate Christ's birth, "that mother of all festivals." Chrysostom asked each person to "leave his home, that we may behold our Lord lying in the manger, wrapped in swaddling clothes, a wonderful and awe-inspiring sight."[4] By that Christmas message, Chrysostom managed to persuade his people to accept the Roman custom of celebrating Christ's birth on December 25.[5]

While we may not agree with Chrysostom that Jesus of Nazareth was actually born on December 25, the point is that he invited his hearers to attend the celebration of the birth of Christ "to behold our Lord." What a glorious invitation! That is what Christmas is all about: namely, that something unique has happened in the history of humankind. God has visited his people and dwelt among them (John 1:14), "taking the very nature of a servant, being made in human likeness" (Phil. 2:7). Who could resist going out and proclaiming the message of invitation to others after having witnessed such an event in one's own life!

3. Epiphany

The term "epiphany" is from the Greek word *epiphaneia,* meaning "appearance" or "manifestation."[6] Theologically, it means the appearance of God to humankind in human form; that is the way in which Jesus Christ manifested himself to the world as the Savior of both the Jews and the Gentiles.

The Epiphany season usually takes four to nine Sundays beginning with January 6, which is the Epiphany. Among the texts associated with the message of the Epiphany season are the visit of the Magi (Matt. 2:1-12); the fulfillment of the Law (Matt. 5:17-20); Christ at twelve years (Luke 2:39-52); Jesus the Lamb of God (John 1:29-34, 35-51); Christ the wisdom and power of God (1 Cor. 1:18-31); oneness of all in Christ (Eph. 2:11-18); Jonah's mission to Nineveh (John 3:1-5); the birth of Samuel (1 Sam. 1:19); and many others.

The message of Epiphany is that down through the centuries, God has manifested himself to his people at many times and in various ways. However, "in these last days," he has done so through his Son, Jesus Christ (Heb. 1:1-2). To this day, God continues unveiling himself in human situations through the reading of Scriptures, preaching, prayer, counseling, and many other ways.

4. Lent

The season of Lent is the 40-day period between Ash Wednesday and Easter Sunday. This period has often been regarded as a time for fasting and penitence. There are six Sundays in the season, with the last one designated as Palm Sunday. The passages associated with Lent include Jesus' teaching on fasting and self-examination (Matt. 6:16-21); the baptism and temptation of Jesus (Mark 1:9-12); the parable of the persistent widow (Luke 18:1-8); the parable of the Pharisee and the tax collector (Luke 18:9-14); rending one's heart (Joel 2:12, 15-17); Ezekiel as a watchman (Ezek. 33:18-23); and many others.

The message of the Lenten season also takes us to the passion story, the heartbeat of the Christian gospel, starting with the Palm Sunday events (Zech. 9:9-12; Phil. 2:5-11; Luke 19:29-40); the Last Supper (Matt. 26:20-25; Mark 14:17-25; Luke 22:14-38); and the Crucifixion (Matt. 27:33-44; Mark 14:22-32; Luke 28:33-43). The passion narrative is believed to have been the first New Testament tradition to be committed to writing.

The Lenten season brings God's people face to face with his unlimited love and mercy once more. Yes, people hear that voice once more: "Father, forgive them, for they do not know what they are doing" (Luke 23:34); or "this brother of yours was dead and is alive again; he was lost and is found" (Luke 15:32); or "Come, see a man who told me everything I ever did. Could this be the Christ?" (John 4:29).

The Lenten season has taught us that people, after being confronted by God's message, do respond. Often they seek forgiveness of their sins from God (Ps. 51); they also seek to be reconciled with their neighbor, brother, or sister (Matt. 5:24). What an opportunity for biblical preaching to dwell on such themes as grace, mercy, forgiveness, and reconciliation in Christ!

5. Eastertide

Easter is the Christian festival celebrating the resurrection of Jesus Christ. The Eastertide includes Easter Sunday and six other Sundays, with the last being designated Ascension Sunday. While the observance of the weekly Easter in commemoration of the resurrection of the Lord started in the days of the apostles (Acts 20:7), the special Easter festival was not celebrated until after New Testament times. The story of Christ's passion and resurrection is enshrined in Paul's Letter to the church in Corinth:

> For what I received I passed on to you as of first importance: that Christ died for our sins according to the Scriptures, . . . that he was raised on the third day according to the Scriptures, and that he appeared to Peter, and then to the Twelve. After that, he appeared to more than five hundred of the brothers at the same time, most of whom are still living, though some have fallen asleep. Then he appeared to James, then to all the apostles, and last of all he appeared to me also, as to one abnormally born. (1 Cor. 15:3-8)

The message of Easter is the message of the resurrection of Jesus Christ from the dead. That message is understood in relation to the whole passion story—the very core of the Christian faith. It is the message of God's victory over evil and death and the exaltation and eternal lordship of Christ. Whereas Adam fell and brought about death because of sin, Jesus Christ won the victory, because "He was delivered over to death for our sins and was raised to life for our justification" (Rom. 4:25). Paul views the event of the resurrection as central to understanding the mystery of salvation in Christ. The resurrection of the dead is to be understood in the light of the resurrection of Christ who was raised from the dead. No wonder Paul writes to the church in Corinth: "And if Christ has not been raised, our preaching is useless and so is your faith" (1 Cor. 15:14).

There are several scriptures that deal with the message of Easter: the empty tomb (Matt. 28:1-10; Mark 16:1-8; Luke 24:1-11); the command to baptize (Matt. 28:16-20); the road to Emmaus (Luke 24:13-35); the appearance of the risen Christ in Jerusalem (Luke 24:36-49); Jesus' appearance to Mary Magdalene (John 20:10-18); Jesus' appearance to his disciples (John 20:19-31); Jesus and the miraculous catch of fish (John 21:1-14); Jesus' reinstatement of Peter (John 21:15-25); and many others.

6. Pentecost

The season of Pentecost consists of 11 to 16 Sundays, beginning with Pentecost Sunday. Citing W. L. Knox as his authority, C. S. C. Williams writes: "Pentecost, originally a harvest festival, had lost its agricultural meaning since Philo's day and had acquired at last a connexion with the giving of the Torah or Law. All that the Torah was to a Jew, Jesus was to Paul and the Holy Spirit to Luke, and more."[7] Originally, Pentecost had been the Jewish harvest festival—the Feast of Weeks, but it eventually came to symbolize the giving of the Torah at Mount Sinai.

Observance of Pentecost as a Christian festival is traced to the third century. For Christians, the festival commemorated the coming of the Holy Spirit. This did not mean that there was no previous experience of the Holy Spirit; it simply means that at Pentecost the disciples, for the first time, experienced the Holy Spirit as the power that Jesus had promised them (Acts 1:8). Some related passages include Peter's address to the crowd (Acts 2:14-39); the healing of a crippled beggar (Acts 3:1-10); Peter and John before the Sanhedrin (Acts

4:1-21); the believer's prayer (Acts 4:23-31); and Stephen's speech before the Sanhedrin (Acts 7:1-59).

Christians also celebrate Pentecost as the birth of the church (Acts 2:1-4). The outpouring of the Holy Spirit upon the disciples as they were gathered in one place on the day of Pentecost brought about the birth of a new community whose conception was embedded in the teaching, crucifixion, resurrection, and ascension into heaven of Jesus Christ. Wherever that message of Christ has been preached in the power of the Holy Spirit, a new fellowship of believers, Jews and Gentiles alike, has come into being. Several well-known scriptures bear witness to this: Peter at Cornelius' house (Acts 10:24-47); Paul in Ephesus (Acts 19:1-7); and others. No wonder some churches observe Pentecost "as a festival of victory in the church."[8] In some denominational traditions, new members were received in the church during this season. "Whitsunday" (which comes from "White Sunday") was often set aside by some churches as the Sunday when candidates were baptized into the church in white robes.[9]

The teaching concerning the Holy Spirit in the life of the African church is an important issue. People rightly believe in the power of the Holy Spirit; at the same time, it is one of the most misunderstood doctrines of the church. Some Christians mistake their personal feelings and emotions for the work of the Holy Spirit. The Pentecost season presents great opportunities for biblical preaching in the African church. As one looks at the enormous rate at which the Christian community is growing in sub-Saharan Africa today, one cannot help thinking that the need for genuine biblical preaching is greater than ever before.

7. Kingdomtide

Kingdomtide (known as Ordinary Time in many church traditions) consists of 13 to 14 Sundays. It is one of the longest seasons, running through the months of September, October, and November.

The emphasis in the message of Kingdomtide is primarily proclamation and the announcement that "Your God reigns" (Isa. 52:7). The Synoptic Gospels bear witness to this great theme of "the kingdom of God" or "the kingdom of heaven" (Matt. 5:3; Mark 1:15; Luke 10:9). The Synoptic Gospels view the whole ministry of Christ Jesus as the fulfillment of the kingdom: for example, Jesus and Beelzebub (Matt. 12:22-28; Mark 3:22-27); Jesus and John the Baptist (Matt. 10:1-10; Luke 7:18-28); Jesus in the synagogue at Nazareth (Luke 4:18-21), and other scriptures. The Synoptic Gospels portray most of the parables as conveying the message of the kingdom. Examples include the parable of the sower (Matt. 13:1-23); the parable of the weeds (Matt. 13:24-30); the parable of the mustard seed (Matt. 13:31-35); the parable of the hidden treasure (Matt. 13:44-45); and the parable of the net (Matt. 13:47-52).

The message concerning the kingdom of God did not begin with the New Testament; we can trace it back to the Old Testament. The message echoes through the words of Isaiah:

> "It is too small a thing for you to be my
> servant
> to restore the tribes of Jacob
> and bring back those of Israel I have
> kept.
> I will also make you a light for the
> Gentiles,
> that you may bring my salvation to
> the ends of the earth." (Isa. 49:6)

The message of the kingdom is proclamation that "your God reigns" because it is God's intention to bring, by means of Israel, both the House of Jacob and the Gentiles under the rule of God. Amos also proclaimed God's kingdom when he cried out:

Away with the noise of your songs!
  I will not listen to the music of your
    harps.
But let justice roll on like a river,
  righteousness like a never-
    failing stream! (Amos 5:23-24)

The message of Kingdomtide is proclamation of the exalted Christ, who invites all nations and all people to a life in which God reigns—the life of love.

Biblical preaching takes every preacher to both Testaments and to all the books of both Testaments. When biblical preaching is guided by the lectionary, it takes the preacher through both easy and difficult passages of the Bible. In the end, biblical preaching, as guided by the church lectionary, will produce preachers who are diligent students of the Bible and congregations that live and thrive on the mission of God.

Notes

1. African Experience of the Bible

1. Bengt Sundkler, *The Christian Ministry in Africa* (London: SCM Press, 1962), pp. 101-3.

2. Preaching and Its Historical Roots

1. Yngve Brilioth, trans. Karl E. Mattson, *A Brief History of Preaching* (Philadelphia: Fortress Press, 1965), p. 18.
2. Ralph G. Turnbull, *Baker's Dictionary of Practical Theology* (Grand Rapids: Baker Book House, 1967), p. 50.
3. Ibid., p. 31.
4. *The Interpreter's Dictionary of the Bible, Vol. R-Z* (Nashville: Abingdon Press, 1962), pp. 478-79.
5. C. S. C. Williams, *The Acts of the Apostles* (New York: Harper and Bros., 1957), p. 99.
6. *Collins Concise Dictionary of the English Language* (London: William Collins Sons, 1978), p. 644.
7. James C. McCroskey, *An Introduction to Rhetorical Communication* (Englewood Cliffs, N.J.: Prentice-Hall, 1968), p. 6.
8. Ibid., p. 3.
9. Ibid.
10. Brilioth, *A Brief History of Preaching*, p. 50.
11. Ibid., pp. 31-39.
12. Ibid.
13. William M. Macartney, *Dr Aggrey* (London: SCM Press, 1948), pp. 81-82.

Notes

3. The Making of the Bible

1. Norman Gottwald, *A Light to the Nations* (New York: Harper and Bros., 1959), p. 20.
2. Ibid., p. 2.
3. C. H. Dodd, *The Bible Tooloy* (Cambridge: University Press, 1962), pp. 33-35.
4. Harrell F. Beck, *Our Biblical Heritage* (Boston: United Church of Christ, 1964), pp. 36-38.
5. William Barclay, *Introducing the Bible* (Nashville: Abingdon Press, 1972), p. 19.
6. Gottwald, *A Light to the Nations*, p. 29.
7. Ibid., p. 30.
8. J. Sherrell Hendricks, Gene E. Sease, Eric Lane Titus, James Bryan Wiggins, *Christian Word Book* (Nashville: Abingdon Press, 1968), p. 24.
9. *The Interpreter's Dictionary of the Bible, Vol. A-D* (Nashville: Abingdon Press, 1962), p. 162.
10. Hendricks, Sease, Titus, Wiggins, *Christian Word Book*, p. 26.
11. Ibid.
12. Ibid., p. 279.
13. *The Interpreter's Dictionary of the Bible, Vol. A-D*, p. 164.
14. Ibid., p. 165.
15. Ibid., p. 521.
16. Adolf Von Harnack, *The Origin of the New Testament* (Covent Garden: Williams and Norgate, 1925)., p. 8.
17. C. F. D. Moule, *The Birth of the New Testament* (New York: Harper and Bros., 1957), p. 58.
18. Ibid., p. 179.
19. Ibid, p. 181.
20. Kurt Aland, *The Problem of the New Testament Canon* (London: A. R. Mowbray and Co., 1962), p. 9.
21. J. Stevenson, *A New Eusebius* (London: S.P.C.K., 1970), p. 122.
22. *The Interpreter's Dictionary of the Bible, Vol. A-D*, p. 527.
23. Stevenson, *A New Eusebius*, p. 146.
24. Barclay, *Introducing the Bible*, p. 43.
25. G. Waddy Polkinghorne, *The Canon of the New Testament* (London: Charles H. Kelly, 1914), p. 112.

4. The Authority of the Bible

1. Dwight E. Stevenson, *In the Biblical Preacher's Workshop* (Nashville: Abingdon Press, 1967), p. 18.
2. In Alan Richardson, ed., *A Theological Word Book of the Bible* (New York: Macmillan, 1966), p. 156.
3. Van A. Harvey, *A Handbook of Theological Terms* (New York: Macmillan, 1964), p. 131.
4. L. Harold DeWolf, *A Theology of the Living Church* (New York: Harper and Bros., 1953), p. 76.
5. Stanley D. Schneider, *As One Who Speaks for God* (Minneapolis: Augsburg Publishing House, 1965), p. 16.
6. J. Robert Nelson, *The Realm of Redemption*, 7th ed. (London: The Epworth Press, 1964), p. 106.

7. Ibid.
8. *The Interpreter's Dictionary of the Bible, Vol. R-Z* (Nashville: Abingdon Press, 1962), p. 251.
9. Stevenson, *In the Biblical Preacher's Workshop*, p. 42.

5. Defining Biblical Preaching

1. William Edwin Sangster, *The Craft of Sermon Construction* (Philadelphia: The Westminster Press, 1950), p. 35.
2. Donald G. Miller, *The Way to Biblical Preaching* (Nashville: Abingdon Press, 1957), p. 26.
3. Ralph G. Turnbull, "The Classification of Sermons," *Baker's Dictionary of Practical Theology* (Grand Rapids: Baker Book House, 1967), p. 59.
4. Miller, *The Way to Biblical Preaching*, p. 22.
5. Merrill R. Abbey, *The Word Interprets Us* (Nashville: Abingdon Press, 1967), p. 39.
6. Jean-Jacques Van Allen, *Preaching and Congregation*, 4th ed. (Richmond: John Knox Press, 1968), p. 7.
7. "Africa: Independent Churches Thrive but Face Hurdles," *Christianity Today* (March 12, 1971), p. 54.
8. John Knox, *The Integrity of Preaching* (Nashville: Abingdon Press, 1957), p. 19.
9. Ibid., pp. 20-21.
10. Turnbull, *Baker's Dictionary for Practical Theology*, p. 68.
11. Ronald E. Sleeth, *Proclaiming the Word* (Nashville: Abingdon Press, 1964), p. 42.
12. John C. Irwin, "The Status of Methodist Preaching," *The Pulpit: A Journal of Contemporary Preaching*, Vol. XXII no. 8 (August 1951), p. 3.
13. Knox, *The Integrity of Preaching*, p. 22.
14. Ibid.

6. Biblical Proclamation in Our Cultural Context

1. John Mbiti, *African Religions and Philosophy* (London: Heinemann, 1969), p. 2.
2. G. Ernest Wright and Reginald Fuller, *The Book of the Acts of God* (Hammondsworth, Middlesex: Penguin Books, 1960).
3. Ibid.

7. Biblical Preaching as a Method

1. Ilion T. Jones, *Principles and Practice of Preaching* (Nashville: Abingdon Press, 1964), p. 80.
2. Henry H. Mitchell, *Black Preaching* (New York: J. B. Lippincott Company, 1970), p. 133.
3. Editorial, *Christianity Today* (March 12, 1971), p. 54.
4. Marshall W. Murphree, *Christianity and Shona* (New York: Humanities Press, 1969), pp. 92-102.

Notes

5. Dwight E. Stevenson, *In the Biblical Preacher's Workshop* (Nashville: Abingdon Press, 1967), p. 146.
6. Harrell F. Beck, *Our Biblical Heritage* (Boston: United Church Press, 1964), p. 21.
7. Oscar Cullmann, ed. A. J. B. Higgins, *The Early Church* (Philadelphia: The Westminster Press, 1956), p. 76.
8. Wallace E. Fisher, *Preaching and Parish Renewal* (Nashville: Abingdon Press, 1966), p. 17.
9. Editorial, *Ministry*, Vol. 6, No. 1 (October 1965), p. 25.

8. Biblical Preaching and the Lectionary

1. J. Sherrell Hendricks, Gene E. Sease, Eric Lane Titus, James Bryan Wiggins, *Christian Word Book* (Nashville: Abingdon Press, 1968), p. 16.
2. Van A. Harvey, *A Handbook of Theological Terms* (New York: Macmillan, 1964), p. 175.
3. Ibid.
4. Oscar Cullmann, ed. A. J. B. Higgins, *The Early Church* (Philadelphia: The Westminster Press, 1956), p. 33.
5. Ibid.
6. Hendricks, Sease, Titus, Wiggins, *Christian Word Book,* p. 94.
7. C. S. C. Williams, *The Acts of the Apostles* (New York: Harper and Bros., 1957), p. 62.
8. Hendricks, Sease, Titus, Wiggins, *Christian Word Book,* p. 226.
9. Ibid.

Indexes

Subject Index

Scripture Index

Indexes